THE THIRD SUNDAY
OF EVERY JUNE

L. E. SCHWALLER

Published by Ten16 Press, an imprint of Orange Hat Publishing

Ten | 16
PRESS

www.orangehatpublishing.com
Wauwatosa, WI

*For my mother, whose love has carried us farther
than she'll ever know, and my father, forever
twenty-nine and a quiet echo in all that I do.*

CHAPTER 1

THE PROS AND CONS OF
NOT WEARING PANTS

St. Louis, MO, 2008

"I'm pregnant," she said, shaking.

Julian was still standing somehow, knees locked, back a rigid plank. The words fell on him and receded back to her, their weight leaving him momentarily catatonic.

"Aren't you going to say something?" She stared at Julian, looking up at him from her spot on the leather sofa, where she sat scrunching her painted toes on the frieze carpet.

It had been a week or more since she had last called and invited him to her place. Such were the unspoken terms of their relationship. There would be distance, a brief hiatus, then a rekindling between the sheets. The bond of sex without emotional attachment.

Her hair, with its nearly black curls, was still damp from a shower and wrapped closely to her thin cheeks, the flyaways brushing gently against skin the color of caramel. In a way, he had missed her in their time apart, and he thought, even in that panicked moment when she first told him he would be a father, of how beautiful she looked.

"You're—you're pregnant?"

"Oh," Maria said, throwing her hair from her face. "You're back! Welcome to the conversation."

It was February, and the salted streets and ground were covered in slush, melting under the warmth of a typical Missouri day that always seems to follow a snowstorm. Trees bowed under the weight of dripping slosh, and their branches sporadically cracked and sprang upward as the hefts of snow slipped free.

"Is it mine?" Julian asked the only thing that felt right, logical.

"Of course it's fucking yours! What the fuck, Julian?"

He knew what was coming next and already regretted having steered the conversation to a place where he would have to lie out of necessity. Out of survival.

"Have you been with anyone else?" she asked, her eyes welling up as if on cue.

"No!" Of course he had.

She hunched forward and pressed her hands together in front of her face the way children do as they pray before bed.

Julian went to her, finally crossing the broad space between them to comfort her. He consoled her with his hands, rubbing her shoulders and kissing her hair. He asked her what they should do, if she would consider any other options. But she wouldn't. She couldn't. She came from a big Mexican family and was too Catholic to do anything else. There were no other options. She would have the child, and it would be disgraceful. That much was certain.

"How did this happen?" he asked, lovingly stroking her hair and silently punishing himself for never bothering to wear a condom with her.

A choking sensation of drowning stirred somewhere deep in his chest. He forced breaths in and out as he reassured her convincingly with shushing and soft coos. He knew Maria could feel his body, a guise of calm and composure. What she couldn't see were his eyes. Those deep brown eyes, wide and searching. A panicked, cornered animal seeking options, flight.

As he held her closely, tenderly, he imagined trying to cradle a bawling infant in his arms. He pictured spittle stains on the shoulders of his tailored suits and then, as he continued to caress Maria's head, his mind drifted to that screaming redheaded brat he had seen at the Galleria with snot crusted over his nostrils, his mouth winged with cherry Kool-Aid stains. No, he decided, he could not be a father. He needed a way out, an escape route. It was then, in that moment of quiet desperation, that he came up with his plan. A strategy so immature and illogical that it had to (and, for a time, did) work. He would, for a lack of better ideas, make a run for it.

Over the next hour or so, he laid the groundwork for his escape, soothing Maria with kisses until she believed that everything would truly be fine. Then they made something like love right there on the beige living room carpet. When they had finished, he put his jeans back on, pulling them over the fresh spots of rug burn on each knee. She walked him to the door, and they embraced again.

"Everything is going to be fine. I'll be there every step of the way," he lied to her once more, his fingertips massaging her back as he held her close and rubbed her nose with his, something his mother had done time and again to show him she meant what she had said.

And with that, he was off, strolling away from her apartment. At first, he had an illusory gait that didn't seem at all panicked. He ambled softly, slowly, so as not to rouse suspicion, even stopping to wave back at her. In that moment, she probably thought he was going to marry her, that he was going to turn into a great father who would love her and provide for her and their child. But sometimes it's the small, unseen things that tell the truth. Those reactions that happen just after you turn away, the moment the line of sight is broken.

Once Julian had guided his car out of her parking lot, merging onto the street and cornering out of sight, he was speeding. He ran stop signs and weaved in and out of traffic until he arrived at my condo.

I heard the burning cry of his tires as he fishtailed around the corner and onto my street. Somehow, I knew it was him. We had been the best of friends, as close as brothers, for as long as I could remember, and I knew, instinctively, that he needed me. The 4.2-liter engine of his A8 could go from zero to sixty in less than six seconds, and I think he tried it out that day, the motor roaring as he rocketed down the straightaway of the condominium complex parking lot where children sometimes played. Screeching to a halt in front of my building, he ran up the stairs to my door without bothering to find a parking spot.

"Brett!" he hollered, banging on the door and struggling for breath. "Brett, open the fucking door!"

I was sitting on the bed with one foot on the plush carpet floor. Despite the urgency in his voice, coupled with my inclinations, I had trouble moving at all. It was a Saturday, and I was hungover. I hadn't left the bedroom all morning and had spent my time lying around with my girlfriend of the moment, Kelly, watching bad television and mangling the sheets with sex before a midmorning catnap. Now, wearing only a pair of tattered soccer shorts, I noticed the mess she had created in my room: designer jeans and a cashmere sweater cast over the back of a chair in the corner, her purse falling open on the floor next to a pair of black heels. I pictured how put together she'd been the night before, looking stunning at dinner and even better for the drinks that ran late into the evening. This disregard for my space, one that likely blossomed from her assumption that sex with me meant something more than the physical act, sent my skin crawling.

As I looked down at Kelly cocooned in the sheets, I listened to Julian call from the front door. The pounding and yelling stirred her awake, and she stretched her arms up out of the sheets that covered everything but her face. Her fingers were bent, palms in an involuntary contraction of muscles, and she yawned deeply. That long blonde hair of hers was tossed and covered her forehead and one of her cheeks. A lock of it ran across the front of her face, stuck in that space between her nose and upper lip, and it looked like a straw-colored Fu Manchu. I knew even then that this day would be our last together.

I got up with some effort and made my way through the condo, scooping up two wineglasses from the coffee table in the living room, one stained with nude lipstick, and setting them on the countertop as I passed by on my way to the front door.

"I'm coming, I'm coming," I said, fumbling with the lock.

Julian burst through the heavy front door the moment I had it cracked. I jumped out of the way as it shot open, the bottom swinging like a scythe over the carpet and nearly crushing the tops of my toes. He stormed in, panting, and I turned to look at him. The sweat glistened on his forehead, and his hair, typically perfectly molded, was in disarray, some strands still tucked behind his ears, the rest falling about his flushed face.

"Is everything all right?" I knew it wasn't but asked because you're supposed to.

Julian walked into my kitchen, his shoes making faint wet squeaks on the graphite-colored tiles. He plucked a glass off the cabinet shelf, filled it with water from the tap, and swallowed every last bit with a gasp.

"She's pregnant," he huffed. "Maria. You know, the one with the dark hair and the perfect body"

I was suddenly aware of how chilled I felt standing there, barely dressed, the February wind whipping up the stairs and striking my bare chest. I shut the front door and walked across the carpet into the kitchen.

"Brett?" Kelly called out with an upward intonation as she peeked her head around the corner, the down comforter wrapped over her torso and covering her naked chest.

"Am I interrupting?" Julian whispered to me, his lip curling into a faint, sly smile. For a moment, he had forgotten his situation because we were, admittedly, still sophomoric despite being nearly thirty.

"Everything's fine. Could you bring me out a shirt, babe?"

Julian sighed, then refilled his glass of water before walking into the living room, plopping down on my black leather club chair and sinking in. He held the water with both hands and stared ahead into the dormant fireplace. I walked over to the wall and flipped the switch. There was a hiss of gas and then a pop as the faux logs were engulfed in flames. The fire breathed onto me, warming my icy legs and pale feet. Kelly walked in, sporting a pair of my running shorts and a sweatshirt. Her mascara was gunked up in the corner of her left eye from sleep and sex. She tossed me the vintage 1982 World Series Championship Cardinals shirt I had paid too much for and wore religiously around the house. I slipped it over my head and led Kelly by the hand to the couch opposite Julian.

"I can't believe this is happening to me," he finally said.

"Are you sure she's pregnant?" I asked.

"Who's pregnant?" Kelly said as she fell into the couch next to me and pulled her knees to her chest.

Julian shot her a look of annoyance that only he and I caught and shared. I noticed he was scruffy, his five o'clock shadow looking as if it were ten or even midnight. He rarely wore facial hair because it grew in uncomfortably coarse. I touched her knee and then pulled her close to me in an attempt to shut her up. Then I rubbed my fingers up and down her thigh. She was warm but unpleasant, her skin prickled and dry in a way I hadn't noticed in the bedroom. It was a little like petting a snake against its scales.

"Are you sure she's pregnant?" I repeated, taking my hand off Kelly's leg.

"I mean, I'm not a fucking doctor," Julian said, "but I don't think she would have gone through all that—telling me I'm going to be a dad, I mean—if she wasn't pretty goddamn sure."

I raised my hands, apologizing, and we sat in silence again.

"Don't be angry at me for asking this," I said, choosing my words carefully, "but are you sure it's yours?"

He nodded. "She seems fairly certain."

"So you asked her?"

He continued to nod.

I felt sorry for him, sympathetic and almost sick to my stomach. And yet, in that moment, I couldn't have been more relieved that this was all happening to him and not me.

"Well, wasn't she on, like, some kind of contraceptive?" I asked.

"That's what I thought," he sat forward, tapping his fingers on the outside of his glass.

"If she was, then she wouldn't be pregnant," I said.

"Not necessarily," Kelly chimed in.

Our eyes darted to her.

"Well," she said, "that stuff isn't a hundred percent effective."

"What?"

She spoke to us deliberately, stressing the words. "You guys know the pill and condoms don't work a hundred percent of the time, right?"

"Uh, no," Julian said, his annoyance palpable now. "I clearly did not know that."

For a moment, I worried that, not seeing how angry he was, Kelly might start to laugh, so I stood up and offered everyone coffee to defuse the situation. As I ground up the beans, breathing in the roast and feeling warm all over, I overheard her talking to Julian, telling him clichéd things like "this could be a blessing in disguise" and all that crap. I brought three cups into the living room and set them on the coffee table along with a short carton of creamer.

"What are you going to do?" I asked, stirring in creamer and watching the steaming coffee swirl until it turned a soft taupe.

"I've been thinking about that," he said as he took a short sip. "And I have an idea. No matter what she says, there are no guarantees the child is mine."

"You could take a paternity test," Kelly interrupted.

"I could," he agreed, "or I could wait it out." Julian seemed to pause for effect. "Maria and I have been together for, what, four months?"

"If that," I said.

"And we weren't too serious," he reminded us. "I've been with a lot of women, and none of them came back pregnant. I've always figured, you know, that it was hard to get pregnant or that I was sterile or something. I think she might be making it up or using it to get to my money. I'm thinking I'll just take a knee and let the clock run out. Maybe it will all blow over. She's a tenacious girl, but nine months is a long time. If push comes to shove—if I am the father, I mean—there's no harm in waiting until the little guy is born. Right?"

I nodded again, knowing deep down that he was wrong, that it didn't make any sense. I wish now that I had said something. I wish I had spoken up when I had the chance. Or at least let Kelly talk instead of silencing her again, this time with a loving pinch to the lower back. But he was in so much pain. I did what any friend, any brother, would do. I took his side, and I stuck by him, never knowing how out of hand things could possibly get.

CHAPTER 2

June 17, 1995

I know it's not a competition, but Julian was first. Not in everything. In fact, I had been the first to feel a girl up. Her name was Ophelia Mason and we were supposed to be watching Jurassic Park at Ronnie's Multiplex in South County when, between slobbery kisses, I leaned over the armrest and reached up under her shirt, sliding my fingers along her stomach. I felt a pain in my ribs, imagining them bruising, even breaking against the pressure of the armrest, but I never ceased my struggle to slip my hand under her bra. Finally, I wriggled my fingers through and pinched her pointed nipple between my finger and thumb. She breathed in deeply, twisted in her seat, and pulled me in to kiss her. At that exact moment, a Tyrannosaurus rex bellowed and crunched through the bones of one of the characters on the screen. Her mouth was wet, her tongue flicking and flopping like an excited Labrador.

I was surprised to find that her breasts didn't feel at all like I expected. They were like mine. A little bigger, sure, and fatty, but it wasn't much different than fondling myself, save for the fact that someone else was there for a change. In the end, my first sexual encounter beyond a kiss, the catalyst for the incipience of my existence as a red-blooded American man, was a disappointment.

But I lied when I told Julian and everyone else about it. I said it was amazing, erotic, although at the time I didn't exactly know the meaning of the word. I told everyone about Ophelia Mason's hard nipples, the feel of her bra, and the heat of her body. From that day forward, she was known only as Oh-Let-Me-Feel-Ya Mason by all the boys at school, which I admit wasn't too clever, but we were, after all, only thirteen.

It was an accomplishment to take pride in. The first boy in our eighth-grade class to touch a girl's breasts. Or maybe I was merely the first to tell everyone about it. Whatever the case, I had started something with my tales at the edge of recess. A revolution of sorts. And we boys became consumed, further obsessed by what lay hidden beneath the fabric of these little girls' Catholic school uniforms because, for the first time, one of us had broken through. Getting some had become an actual, attainable possibility, which led to countless iterations of "How did you do it, man?" So, I wrote notes, instructions guiding the other boys on how to feel a girl up, publishing lengthy directions on how to unhook a bra. These manuals looked something like the assembly instructions of an Ikea shelving unit, little doodles showing the detailed workings of the bra hooks and eyes and pointing out the structural weaknesses. The best of which included a step-by-step process:

1. Reach around her side to the small of her back.

2. Move your fingers up, then slip them under the back strap of her bra.

3. Pinch both sides of the clasp between finger and thumb until it pops open.

4. Enjoy!

For the record, I didn't actually know how to do this to a girl. No, at the time I had learned by putting on my mom's bra and standing with my back to the mirror. Regardless, within weeks, everyone was copping a feel. Over the following months and years, the emerging transition from boy to manhood became a kind of arms race, a game of swelling numbers and accomplishments.

"Did you hear Alex Kraemer felt up Christina Kleuter on Friday, and then Sarah Hern on Saturday?"

"Sluts!"

"I heard Matt Carter sucked Lacy Martin's tits!"

"What tits?"

"Wes stink-fingered Geena Fuller!"

And so on.

Needless to say, Julian had found his niche, the purpose of his young life emerging in the pursuit of women. As I look back on things, his motivation was interesting but not surprising. Going back to when we were kids watching 80s action movies or Cardinals games on KLPR, we'd always talked about our heroes and how they were men, *real men*. And these men, at least the ones Julian was drawn to, didn't have steady girlfriends or longtime wives. They were rambling men.

Landing women was also, much to the frustration of his friends, natural for Julian. He was an attractive boy, dark and handsome even as an early teenager, without even a hint of the awkwardness that the rest of us exemplified in spades. But his mother was truly the secret to his success. She kept him stylishly dressed and unwittingly taught him how to seduce, all those years of grooming and lessons in politeness molding him into an artist of sorts capable of knowing women, what they needed to hear and feel. His mother had created a monster of unchecked male promiscuity without ever comprehending the enemy she was making for her fair sex. And it was in Julian's basement, back in June of 1995, when he was merely fourteen years old, that the spoils of those talents were first realized and consummated.

His mother had essentially pimped for him by picking up sweet Heather Gibbs and delivering her to Julian. Heather was blonde and cute, with pink cheeks and freckles on her nose, and she thought Julian was her boyfriend. It was afternoon, and he told me later that she smelled like strawberry ChapStick. Julian's mother gave the two of them all the privacy they needed, parked in front of the big-screen television in their dimly lit downstairs rec room. The lemonade and popcorn she had laid out on the coffee table for them was like an aphrodisiac, the movie foreplay. To this day, I can't understand how she was so unconscious of the role she had played.

Neither Julian nor Heather Gibbs had planned on losing their virginity that day, at least not as far as I know, though Julian was certainly prepared. The two of us had stashed condoms everywhere we could think of for months. For instance, he had ripped the lining under the basement couch, a leather convertible, and shoved a few rubbers inside just in case he might need them.

According to Julian, the afternoon he had spent with Heather Gibbs was, for lack of a better word, perfect. They were fourteen, scarcely developed, inexperienced, though in the moment it all somehow just felt right. Once he got inside of her, he has always said, everything else just slipped away. She was lithe, all smooth limbs and soft skin, her legs spread wide apart as she murmured single syllables that were both moans and whimpers of pain. And then, within a few minutes, it was all over.

Afterward, they dressed and then snuggled on the couch, watching movies and eating popcorn. He never asked her over to his basement again. Last I heard, she was married with three kids and living in North County.

"I did it!" he shouted, jumping off his bicycle and pushing it into the grass of my front yard as he rushed up to me that summer evening. He was panting from riding as hard and fast as he could to tell me the news. "I finally did it."

"It?" I was out front in the driveway, rinsing caked grass flakes off our lawnmower with a hose in the fleeting light of dusk. Those were my summer Saturdays: mowing the yard for my mother each weekend from the age of ten until twentysomething, when I could finally afford a lawn service for her. Some boys would go to the pool or fuck girls on their basement couches on the weekend afternoons of summer. I, on the other hand, would push the mower back and forth until it got dark, worrying about losing a toe, sneezing from the pollen and the smell of cut grass, and having every little severed blade of green lawn stick to my sweaty legs.

"Yes, it!" His smile broadened to the point of breaking.

"Bullshit." I couldn't believe it. To my knowledge, he had never lied to me, but I still couldn't believe it.

Julian nodded, looking as if he might burst with excitement at any moment as he pulled the soiled condom from his pocket to prove himself. Seeing it made me queasy. It was withered and slimy like a snake that had been run over in the street. I looked at Julian. His face was bright, and he was happy, happier than I had ever seen anyone in my entire life. He was practically bouncing.

"Who?"

"Gibbs," he said, gyrating his hips as if he were still humping her.

"But she's so nice." I had no interest in Heather, but in that moment, I felt jealous of him, as though he had somehow betrayed me.

"Not anymore," he said.

"How did you do it?"

He laughed and turned to watch a set of headlights wash down the street, then walked to the end of the driveway and tossed the condom into the storm drain at the curb.

"I mean, like, what positions and stuff?" I wanted to know everything.

"I was just, I dunno, kinda on top of her," he said proudly as he wiped the spermicidal lubricant from the condom onto his khaki shorts. "It was awesome. Unbelievable, really."

I asked him question after question that evening, questions that continued and were repeated for weeks to follow. It was a countless cavalcade of hows and wheres. I wanted to know the sensations. I wanted to feel the inside of Heather Gibbs and smell her on my fingers, if only vicariously through my best friend.

"It felt so great. It was awesome. She's unbelievable," was all he would ever say, and to this day, he has never admitted anything to the contrary.

Over the next few weeks, as I obsessed over Heather Gibbs and the afternoon Julian spent inside of her, I felt like I was dying. And each time I paused on my walk past the wrought-iron fence of the public pool, my soul ached as I ogled Heather and all the other neighborhood girls in the flowered bikinis that covered the important parts of their shimmering bodies as they splashed in the water or sunbathed on deckchairs. I wanted one, just one, all to myself. I didn't care which. And I was convinced that if Julian was ready, I was too.

CHAPTER 3

May 18, 1981

Julian and I were born six months apart. He was a May baby, a springtime joy that his parents welcomed from the moment of conception. They had been trying for almost three years, trying for a son, and in the end, they were so excited by his imminent birth that they couldn't choose a name.

"Something will come to us," his father had said, his outstretched fingers walking along the bulge of his wife's belly.

"What makes you so sure?"

"A feeling, I guess," he assured her. "Whenever he's born, we'll know. We'll just know."

Julian's parents had been trying for so long. They were madly in love and eager, and their son was a welcomed bundle that accompanied bluebirds and warm tree buds when his mother gave birth in St. Mary's off Bellevue. On the birth certificate, his parents named him after his father, Gabriel, agreeing that he was no Gabriel, yet putting something down temporarily until a better, more fitting name came to them.

Then they took him home, to the home on Gray Avenue, just a few blocks from where I would soon be. Gabriel laid him down into the crib and ran his long finger gently down his nameless infant son's cheek.

The boy who would be Julian was swaddled in the same blanket Gabriel had been wrapped in as an infant, the blanket that marked his heritage, having survived some thirty years and a trip across the Atlantic. And it was then, as he looked from the boy to the blanket and back to the boy and was reminded of all he had come from and all that lay ahead, that Gabriel decided there was no ordinary name befitting the perfectly shaped nose and lips that favored this boy's mother, nor the eyes that matched his. No, this boy couldn't be known by the name of his father, or his father's father. It didn't matter what the birth certificate read; he would never be called that. This boy was his son, but he was not a Gabriel; he didn't look like a Gabriel. This boy, his boy, looked like something else, a name he couldn't quite put his tongue on.

Their home on Gray Avenue was beautiful and clean, modest in size. Two stories of red brick with blue shutters, cozy and inviting in the shivering months, open and airy for every other season. The floors were a dark, polished hardwood that stretched from wall to wall, and the main floor smelled of potpourri. It was the sort of house you'd like to wake up to on Christmas morning.

Gabriel Reyes—Julian's father, that is—was a proud man. He was a dark, first-generation American whose family was from Talavera de la Reina, a suburb of Madrid. Gabriel's mother and father were part of a minute, though prominent, group of liberals who, having been exiled by Franco, immigrated to the United States. How or why they came to Missouri remains one of those mysteries that sprout up when we forget to ask our aging relatives to share their stories.

Julian's father had been raised as Spanish as he could be in St. Louis, which is to say he was raised Catholic like everyone else in the city and could speak Spanish if he chose to. He was a strong man, forgoing much of high school to work as a bricklayer. To this day, Julian often points out the buildings of the Anheuser-Busch brewery that his father helped build. Gabriel was handsome, rugged, with big hands and long black hair that fell over his ears. The star of his high school baseball team, he had caught the eye of Julian's mother. The two fell in love and became high school sweethearts, defying their parents, which, given their backgrounds, was a rarity at the time.

When Julian was born, his father had just turned thirty, and the day after his nameless son had been brought home, Gabriel returned to work. He kissed his wife on the mouth as she held their infant son and set off.

It was raining, and he would likely be sent home from a jobsite in the Central West End, but he went in because that's how men with integrity lived (or at least that's how Grandpa Mike would always tell it later). Gabriel wasn't five miles from their home when the sedan to his right changed lanes on old Highway 40 near Hampton Avenue and hydroplaned. The rear quarter panel of his pickup truck, a '78 Dodge, was clipped, and he was sent spinning out of control and slammed into the guardrail. His neck snapped, killing him instantly. And so it went. The infant Julian was left fatherless and without a name before he could even know the difference.

CHAPTER 4:

AN AMERICAN FAMILY BUSINESS

I guess I didn't know how far Julian would really take things. As his best friend, I couldn't abandon him when he decided to run from Maria. So I stayed by his side like the wife of some politician caught writing a check to a prostitute. To be honest, I didn't take the time to actually think about what was happening. Maria's pregnancy was a surprise, and, at the time, I couldn't see pregnancy and fatherhood as anything more than an unwanted accident. I had never sat down to have that conversation with Julian, to actually talk with him about being a father. I thought it was womanly to want children—marriage and children being a kind of trap that men are pulled into.

Julian stuck with his plan to wait it out, assuming that Maria was either lying or that the child couldn't possibly be his. Perhaps he took things a bit too far when he changed his phone number and moved, but once you've set yourself on a path of silence and support, it's difficult to speak up. Plus, Julian's new house on Cricklewood Place in Frontenac was gorgeous. Surrounded by maple and oak trees, his place was a townhome in a complex of four that had been built out of russet brick to look like a Dutch Colonial, except the roof wasn't steep and instead had a rather gently sloped apex with brown thatching accented with hunter ivy and moss.

"I had always planned to move out here," he claimed as part of his newfound pretense that he wasn't on the lam.

In honor of this new, lush suburbia dotted with manicured flowerbeds, Julian bought an overpriced grill and fancy patio furniture, along with a riding mower even though they contracted a lawn service. There were signs for the Neighborhood Watch, and each time I pulled up, I expected a golden retriever to run into the front drive and start licking me. Even though he refused to acknowledge his unborn son, Julian was inadvertently morphing into a suburban dad, and I made sure he received an endless cascade of shit for it.

Once he had changed his address and phone number, "Phase 2" began, and Julian fell into his work. It might seem a bit odd given the number of times they'd slept together, but Maria didn't know anything more about him than his name, old telephone number, and former address, which meant she couldn't trace him in any of the traditional ways. Their relationship had been superficial, after all, for which Julian was only partially to blame. In the end, it was easy for him to slip away after he walked out of her apartment that February day. To her, I'm sure it seemed as if he had simply vanished, like one of those mobsters who goes out for a pack of cigarettes and never returns. I think Julian was counting on her thinking the worst.

As for me, although I had met her a few times, she only knew me as Brett. We had double-dated and drank together. I had danced with her once and remembered her as graceful on her long legs, her toes always painted a deep and classic cardinal red. And she was perpetually tan, hued similarly to Julian, though her ethnicity ran closer to the surface than his. But those few occasions out had been the extent of it. She knew nothing of what I did or where I lived, which meant I couldn't serve as a lead, and even if she had managed to track me down, at the time I liked to think I wouldn't crack under interrogation or even torture.

To hedge his bets even further, Julian changed his entire routine. For the first time in his life, he actually worked, nearly doubling the amount of time he typically spent in the office as he logged nine-hour days at Jack Lally and Sons Realty and Development Company. In fact, the office on Finney and North Newstead in Vandeventer became his sanctuary, his refuge. He would park in the garage, occasionally lunching with me, but rarely anywhere near University City, the neighborhood where Maria lived.

Lally and Sons was a family business that had been passed down from his mother's side. The Lallys were Black Irish from County Kerry with black hair and eyes. The result, when intermingled with the Spanish of his father, was racial ambiguity. Perpetually tanned, Julian called it.

The birthright that accompanied a mother born with the last name Lally had opened with a story like that of so many other Irish American families, when Julian's forebears had immigrated to America in the 1840s, singing:

So pack up your sea-stores, consider no longer,

Ten dollars a week is not very bad pay,

With no taxes or tithes to devour up your wages,

When you're on the green fields of America.

"It was too black and dirty," Julian's grandfather Michael had said, speaking with an air of nostalgia as if he had come off the boat in New York City. "There wasn't a green speck of open land to be found." I listened to the man as if he were my own grandfather, having spent more Christmas Eves and Thanksgiving dinners with Julian's family than my own.

The Lallys, Julian's great-great-grandparents, went searching for those green fields, moving as far west as St. Louis. The reasons for settling in that particular city have never been questioned or even discussed as far as I can tell. At first, the family prospered in a blue-collar, salt-of-the-earth sort of way, pocketing themselves with other Irish in "the Patch," a slum north of downtown that was, by and large, run by Irish gangs. I imagine the tenement housing was covered with as much dark soot as the old Bronx, but at least you could have traveled out, a few minutes away from the neighborhood, to see the open fields for which the family had longed.

It is said that many native St. Louisians would start or join in on riots in "the Patch," trying to drive the Irish out of town, though none of those stories of bigotry and violence were shared on the holiday evenings I spent with Julian's family. Eventually, things in "the Patch" calmed down, as they did across the rest of the country, and by the time Julian's great uncle Jack was old enough to enlist in the army, the family had become established, patriotic, American even.

Jack was twenty-one then and left behind a younger brother who was too young to fight, the younger brother who would become Julian's grandfather. Great Uncle Jack was strong and fast, star of the high school football team, a natural infantryman and member of the renowned 505th Parachute Infantry Regiment of the 82nd Airborne, who, after six weeks of training in North Africa, invaded Sicily.

Julian's grandfather told us the story secondhand. We were on the back porch of Julian's house after a family barbecue, and Grandpa Mike was drunk. He delivered the manly war heroics of his older brother to two eager nine-year-old boys as if they were his own, explaining first that Great Uncle Jack was part of Operation Mincemeat, a strategy of misdirection in which the Allies had floated a corpse in a British uniform with a briefcase of fake plans handcuffed to his bloated, waterlogged wrist so it would drift ashore in Spain. The paratroopers, Jack among them, were dropped in a few minutes after midnight on July 10, 1943. This was the first regimental-sized combat jump in history, and Jack, along with nearly all the U.S. paratroopers, ended up far from their intended drop zones. Most never made it to their rallying points, Grandpa Mike explained.

As fate would have it, Jack met up with and fought alongside the British contingent of the invasion and was one of ninety soldiers to hold Ponte Grande Bridge for nearly fifteen hours from Italian troops. The battle went on through the night and into the next day, and it was ten o'clock in the morning when Jack was shot in the stomach. The bullet, a ricochet, had skipped off a mound of rocks and sunk into his belly as he ducked behind a bunker to reload his Thompson. He was dragged far to the rear of the British troops, and the medic gave him a Squibb, a morphine syrette that looked like a little silver tube of toothpaste. The medic punctured the seal and stuck him in the stomach, giving him the first taste of thousands. The bullet was lodged deep in Jack's abdomen, and there was little the young medic could do for him during the middle of a firefight, so he showed him how to administer the morphine to himself and shoved a fistful of Squibbs, enough to kill him, into his hands.

Jack bled and bled. The first shot of morphine should have knocked him out, but he claimed that he could remember screaming for hours until he realized no one was listening. He stuck himself with another collapsible tube injector of morphine, then another and another.

When the British troops surrendered, Jack was forgotten in a grove of juniper trees. The British medic, a man whose name he never learned, had been captured or killed by one of the Napoli Division who had overtaken the British troops, and Jack was left to bleed to death.

He slept, slipping in and out of consciousness for the next six hours as he slowly leaked. His hair was wafted about his sweating face, his body cooled by the arid winds of the Sicilian summer. Then, at dusk, he was discovered by the first group of troops to reach Vizinni, the nearby town that Allied soldiers had managed to capture by the second day of the assault on Sicily.

Jack was unconscious when they found him, dreaming that he was floating on his back in a moonlit ocean. His mouth was cracked and dry, his head resting on the ground, arms stretched out to either side, palms flat and facing the sky. The soldier who found him, a man named Godfrey, said that at first Jack looked like a man taking a nap, resting after a hard day's work. Godfrey realized quickly that this man lying in the dirt was alive, so he, along with another soldier, carried Jack on a makeshift gurney to the battalion camp set up outside of Vizinni.

The doctors went to work on him, removing the slug from his gut, a souvenir he'd kept for some fifty-five years until he got drunk one Christmas and, mistaking him for one of his own grandchildren, gave it to Julian.

Over the weeks during which he recovered, stories of his heroism spread across the front. Even General George S. Patton came to visit Uncle Jack, the hero who had survived the daring airdrop and losing battle for Ponte Grande Bridge, a unified front with the British troops fighting for freedom against the fascists.

Uncle Jack had admitted later that he was too tired to shake Patton's hand firmly, like a man. He also said that the legendary general bore very little resemblance to the famous biopic, one that Julian and I loved because nothing could epitomize the masculine, the warrior, like a general ornamented with medals and standing in front of an American flag backdrop to rally his troops with lines such as: "We're not just going to shoot the bastards; we're going to cut out their living guts and use them to grease the treads of our tanks!" From the La-Z-Boy, a whiskey in his hand, Uncle Jack berated Julian and me, his gruff voice sounding ironically like George C. Scott's, because it was like watching a caricature, a cartoon of a great man. "A goddamn travesty," as he called it.

Julian's great uncle Jack had spent the rest of his tour of duty in the hospital at Vizinni, suckling morphine and sleeping with nurses whenever they could pull him from the haze he tried to keep himself in. Benumbed by the near-endless supply he scored from doctors by complaining of phantom pains, he lost weight and grew gaunt. Then, after four months of desperately and comically trying to keep himself in the ward as if something out of Heller, he was deemed healthy enough to be released from the hospital. Awarded a Silver Star, an honor that eighty-four soldiers in the 82nd Airborne received, and a Purple Heart, he was then sent home to America a hero, a hero painfully and secretly addicted to morphine.

Jack's trip home on a boat back to the States opened with three full days and nights of sweats and vomiting. However, by the time he landed in New York, he was clean and well-rested and soberer than he would be for the rest of his life. His kid brother Michael, Julian's grandfather, a dark-haired man with a thin face pocked with acne scars who always laughed and gave Julian candy when he visited, met him at the pier. Grandpa Mike had become something of a man while his brother was away. As the two took the long train ride to St. Louis, where the family eagerly waited to welcome their war hero, Michael overwhelmed his older brother's ears with get-rich-quick schemes, explaining that the money he had saved working for a construction crew in downtown St. Louis would be enough to get them started in their own business. But Uncle Jack, never much for listening to his younger brother, simply fell asleep with his head against the window.

Jack was a war hero, a neighborhood legend, and citywide celebrity who never again paid for a drink. Nobody knew of his nightmares, his dreams of Squibbs, and his longings to be rocked to sleep every night by the black ocean waves bathed in moonlight. In time, he moved up north with a beauty queen named Lillian. She had been Miss St. Louis County, and she eventually became Julian's great aunt, though she died before he ever had the chance to meet her.

Morphine had long since been made illegal for domestic use, and Jack, afraid to ruin his reputation by risking scandal, discovered that sour mash whiskey numbed him nearly as effectively. He'd chug himself to sleep, burning his esophagus to the point where doctors would later warn him that he was going to corrode his way right through it.

When Michael approached his older brother again in March of '46, his plans sounded less like scheming and more like a business proposition that might actually work. He had dreamt of it as he and St. Louis grew up together. Having done the math, Michael figured out what this country would need most. The war was over, and the world had changed. There was a dream emerging that would be America. This nation would realize itself as a place of wealth and prosperity. It would be a country of those who have, a rarity to have not. Milk and honey would become beer and hot dogs, and baseball would rule the land. But this American dream wasn't something that would just appear. It had to be built. And those with the foresight to get in early would reap the profits. So he again approached his older brother, who was three days gone in the midst of a binge and sleeping on the cold floor of his apartment kitchen. Michael shook his older brother. Jack was awake as he could be at eight o'clock in the morning, his face crusted to the linoleum with dried slobber. It didn't take a whole lot of convincing. Jack had become a junkie, and it had robbed him of any will to disagree, so halfway through his brother's speech, he nodded his head in agreement, then ran to the bathroom to vomit.

The plan was simple enough: Make the American dream possible by building houses for everyone who had returned home from the war. Michael had a magazine clipping of cookie-cutter houses, these things called suburbs. He was convinced this country was on the cusp of an eruption. America was on top of the world, and Michael knew just how they could make some money off it. The man also knew how to market, and it was his suggestion that they name the business after the family hero and eldest brother: Jack Lally and Sons Realty and Development Company. The "Sons" bit was something they figured they should tack on for when they had children.

They made a fortune buying up land out west of St. Louis and then subcontracting companies to build subdivisions. Through the fifties and sixties, they raked money in hand over fist and bought the office building in Vandeventer. Michael ran everything, the genius behind it all, while his brother drank, rarely doing more than taking suppliers, clients, and contractors out for cocktails or lunch. Jack was the face of the family business, while Michael ran the day-to-day. And it was then, finally, after two world wars and only a few generations in America, that the Lallys had realized their dream by toiling homes out of the green fields west of St. Louis.

However, there were no jobs for the Lally women. Even the secretarial work was off-limits. So when Julian's mother was old enough, she went to college, earning a degree she'd never need, and married Julian's father. Then, after Julian's father passed away, he and his mother were provided for. Julian's uncles had taken over the company, buying and selling property at astronomical profits, and by the time Julian turned eighteen, he was given an office facing Finney Avenue. And though Julian's grandfather had simply had an idea, an inkling of something that might make the family rich, he had somehow stumbled upon a talent that all the Lally boys possessed. It was in their blood to know land, what it was worth, and what it could be.

Grandpa Mike had looked at the fields out west and seen gold in those rolling green hills. He then built a community out there, a place for patriots and heroes returning home from the war. Julian's uncles— Jack's sons—had the gift too. They could look at a hole, a dump of gravelly nothing in the middle of the city, and picture a tower of condominiums. And then there was Julian's generation, he and his cousin, Jack II, who would drive through the rundown neighborhoods and see clean streets and remodeled buildings.

Julian was scarcely twenty-six when he took over full partnership in the company. He and his cousin could see the money that could be made in the Central West End, so they bought up property, blocks and blocks of houses that were crumbling. Then, house by house, street by street, they had them remodeled and resold, skyrocketing the prices of the closest neighborhoods so that the poorer families would have to move. They were given tax breaks by the city to practice their particular brand of gentrification and made more than they knew what to do with. By buying old homes and paying contractors to rebuild them, they could resell everything at an exorbitant profit to trendy and rich white people who were tired of the bourgeoisie suburbs, which had once, ironically enough, been dreamt of and built by Julian's grandfather. Julian sold what he and his company called "the lavish city life" to people who were no more conscious of those they had displaced than a bulldozer is of an anthill.

When the proverbial shit hit the fan and Maria confronted Julian with her pregnancy, he essentially barricaded himself up in his office in Vandeventer, an older building, the façade of which reminded me of a dentist's office. By disappearing from the social scene and falling into work, he hoped to create the impression that he—and certainly his money—had dropped off the face of the Earth.

"The baby probably isn't even mine," he said a handful of times as part of his ongoing effort to justify things. I always felt obliged to simply nod. After all, I told myself, our friendship was worth more than a little quibble over paternity.

However, it was about that time when I first caught myself counting the weeks and months, calculating Maria's first trimester then her second in my head. Time was ticking by, but nothing had changed. We worked and worked, lying low, as Julian called it. Six months had gone by without so much as a word or an inkling that Maria was even looking for Julian. His plan was working exactly as he had intended. But then the baseball season started, and we couldn't stay out of sight any longer.

It was a Thursday, and after work we started the night at Vin De Set, a rooftop bar and bistro, before heading on to Ozzie Smith's sports bar to watch the Cardinals play. We drank beer and talked of life and work and women.

Then, at some time around the seventh inning, I noticed a television hanging above the bar. The only one not playing the game. It displayed a presidential hopeful as he delivered a speech. The closed captioning was choppy and erratically scrolling across the bottom of the screen with typos, but I read on, following his address in which he ridiculed Black men like himself for being bad fathers. He quoted an article from the sixties that called Black families a "tangle of pathology." The message somehow struck a chord with me as this politician was chastising men for abandoning their own children, creating and reinforcing a system of poverty and hardships that need not exist. He was rebuking not just his own race but men everywhere, telling them to step up and take responsibility. I was two feet away from my best friend and couldn't bring myself to say a word.

I turned briefly to Julian, who was staring intently at the game, then motioned to the waitress and held up my empty bottle and pointed to it, beckoning her to bring another. The Cardinals scored and everyone cheered and, for the moment, I chose to forget about it all.

CHAPTER 5

December 1, 1980

As it turns out, I was conceived on April Fools' Day. It was a Tuesday evening after my parents had finished up with their night classes and tipped back a few. I suppose the whole thing happened on that same dingy couch in the living room of their apartment where my mother, some three weeks after my conception, decided to break the news to my father. The two were in college, young and unmarried, and she likely thought they would be together forever.

Following my father's great exodus, something changed in my mother, and the transition could be noticed readily in the photographs that had been taken before and then after I was born. In time, as she weathered her pregnancy as a twenty-year-old single woman, she grew hard and shed her childlike femininity. With each passing day, as her belly swelled and I morphed from a Sea-Monkey into something that looked like an alien, she too began to grow and change, eventually evolving into a fiercely independent and strong woman.

My mother had always been a voracious reader with an ability to retain anything and everything, all qualities that I came, in time, to share. But as I grew inside of her, she found herself admiring different characters, ones that she had previously skimmed past during a perhaps more immature reading. Where she had once adored Helen of Troy, so classically beautiful that a war might be fought over her, my mother now grew to love the less feminized, more independent women of literature. After my father left, she despised women like Helen, beautiful women, chastising them as possessions of men, unable to live without the care of a man. Instead, she now canonized characters like Brett Ashley from Hemingway's *The Sun Also Rises* and Jenny Fields, that misunderstood feminist demagogue and mother of T.S. Garp.

Later, she fell in love with Offred from Atwood's dystopian *The Handmaid's Tale*. Then, during her classics phase, she wept aloud when Anna Karenina threw herself in front of that train, sobbing as if it were the suicide of a dear friend. This was followed shortly by *Flaubert and Madame Bovary*, and I can remember how she even tried in vain to explain the line "Madame Bovary, c'est moi" to me. I was twelve at the time and had no idea what the hell she was going on about.

When my father abandoned us, my grandparents expected their daughter on their doorstep at any moment. But she never sought out help or asked for money. Instead, she scoured the classified ads for a cheap room, picked one at random, and moved the two of us—me still in her stomach and looking a bit like an amorphous blob with nubs of arms and legs sticking out—into a house with an old woman in Des Peres.

Gloria Brown, a widow with no children who had been left by her husband to die alone in their four-bedroom colonial, took out an ad in the paper to fill some of the empty space in her home. She was in her early sixties and breathed Karelia Slims by the carton as she wandered from room to room throughout the afternoons in search of housework or some random project to kill time until it was an acceptable hour to pour a drink.

Then my mother and I arrived, the only people who were—or would be—interested in the rooms she had to rent. Gloria took to my mother immediately. Progressive despite her age and generation, she sympathized with my mother's situation, going so far as to insist that she couldn't ask for any rent for the room.

Life in Des Peres was, according to my mother, pleasant, and the two women lived in harmony under those high ceilings as they walked on the creaking wood floors and talked at the kitchen table into the wee hours. They developed a relationship, my mother finding something in Gloria's affection and wide smile that she had never had with my father. They laughed together every day, my mother has said, and Gloria beamed with an infectious anticipation for my birth as they pored over baby books and bounced names off each other. Gloria immediately filled and overflowed the void left by my father. My mother claims that Gloria was more supportive, with a greater patience and understanding during morning sickness than my father, or any man for that matter, could have ever been. In many ways, Gloria served as partner to my mother, and I was to be their first child.

With time, my mother started to show, but she kept up with all of her studies, working nightly at the kitchen table while Gloria fixed supper or leaned against the sink and smoked. Those months awaiting my arrival were, my mother has told me, some of the happiest of her life.

I had gestated twenty-two weeks when, hands clasped together tightly, Gloria and my mother watched the technician perform an ultrasound.

"Do you want to know the sex of your baby?"

"I already do." My mother smiled.

She was convinced, certain of what I was to be. Gloria and my mother had read books, channeled soothsayers, consulted the Chinese Gender Chart, and played with old wives' tales. They noticed my mother was carrying high, wasn't craving salt, and suffered morning sickness often. The two even broke down the vulgar details of where she and my father were when I was conceived, the angle he was inside of her, how exactly he came...

One evening they conducted a test just to be sure. My mother, who was a good eight months along, lay on her back on the old rug in the middle of the living room, wearing nothing but a bra and a pair of sweatpants, while Gloria, who had tied her old wedding ring to a piece of string, stood over her and suspended the ring a few inches from her belly. The two held their collective breath and watched the way it moved. According to the old wives' tale, if the ring had simply swayed back and forth, it meant she was to have a boy. However, on that night, the ring moved in uneven circles, orbiting my mother's stretched navel. It was in that moment that their unscientific tests and feminine intuitions all culminated in one certain, unwavering truth: I was going to be a girl.

Finally, after two hundred and sixty-six joyous days of being anticipated, I was ready for my big entrance. My mother's water broke in the shower, so there was no mess. The contractions were slow, and she was barely dilated. Apparently, I was in no real rush.

Gloria accompanied her in the delivery room, leaving my grandparents to wait in the lobby. There was no word from my father. For all anyone has ever known, he simply lost his footing on this Earth and drifted off as the rest of us continued spinning around. My mother hadn't attempted to pursue him, having shed her last tear on that old couch where I had been conceived.

I was to be her life now, the purpose behind living well and finishing school. I, Brett Corwin, was given her last name instead of my absentee father's. As for my first name, Brett Ashley is the eponym, as I was named after the strong and easy Hemingway character who will forever be pretty to think of. Better than a boy named Sue, I guess.

The fact that I could have had a penis had not occurred to my mother. She was ready to be a mother, sure, but never the mother of a son. Up until that very moment, she had prepared herself to raise a stalwart and beautiful daughter to be a modern Brett Ashley, feminine and independent.

My mother pushed and pushed, exhausting herself as she labored for nearly twenty hours, her loose hair matted to her cheeks, sweat dripping from her chin. Then, finally, at sunrise on a Monday morning, as a wet snow was falling about the hospital windowpanes, I was pulled into this world, held squirming in the capable hands of an obstetrician. I was smeared with afterbirth and screaming as I writhed in his hands like some slippery, barking catfish he had just reeled in. Gloria looked on as I was handed to the midwife, and she began to tear up, a new mother at sixty-three.

"It's a boy!" the midwife said, wrapping me in a blanket.

"Are you sure?" My mother leaned forward between her knees to look, the balls of her arched feet still planted in the stirrups. "Can you check again?"

CHAPTER 6

August 25, 1990

Julian's father, Gabriel Reyes, had abandoned his son as my father had abandoned me. To be fair — or unfair, depending on how you approach these things — it was the rain and underinflated tires of the rival sedan on Highway 60 that Wednesday morning in 1981 that had robbed Julian of a father rather than the fear that had deprived me of mine.

Despite aching to keep a little more of him, Julian's mother respected the wishes of her late husband and did not name her son after his father— or, at least, she didn't call him by his father's name. She had wanted to desperately, of course, and thought that perhaps by calling him Gabriel she might save that name and savor it on the pout of her lips, as if hearing it called out might soften the heartache. But she resisted and tried, for nearly a week as she grieved, to pick a name for her child that her late husband might have approved of, scouring *The Big Book of Baby Names* and scrawling handwritten lists of possibilities, pages and pages, only to throw them out. Then, on the seventh day following her husband's death, after seven long days and nights of grieving and searching, she came across the name Julian. She found it melodious, imagining (strangely) that it was similar in a way to her late husband's. And so, one late afternoon as he suckled at her breast, she asked.

"My beautiful child," she soothed. "What do you think of the name Julian?"

He smacked, eagerly nursing at her.

"Do you like it? You look like a Julian. It is the only name I can think of that is nearly as beautiful as you are."

He closed his eyes, exhausted and full from feasting, and his head nestled back into her arms as he drifted off to sleep. She covered herself and laid him into his crib, smiling as she whispered his name over and over again into his ear.

"Julian, my perfect Julian," she cooed.

It was a soft and mellifluously beautiful name that Gabriel likely would have never chosen.

"Julian." She ran her finger down his soft cheek as he slept. "My sweet, beautiful Julian." She was satisfied.

During the years that followed, Julian and his mother lived together in a harmony that might have existed had he never left her womb. His mother didn't work, and instead they were supported comfortably by the dividends of the Lally family business. Julian's grandfather and great uncle considered a widowed mother and fatherless son to be like any of the youths and women in the family. The company had been built and run solely by men, and it would care for them with comforts far exceeding the realms of necessity, at least until Julian grew old enough for the crown and keys to the kingdom.

Julian and his mother spent day and night together. She taught him to count and recognize his colors. She cooked for him and nuzzled against him at night, petting his head until he fell asleep and she could slip away to her own room. In fact, there were many mornings in which Julian would wake to find his mother still in his bed.

They existed together in this fashion, almost as one, until the moment Julian Reyes was dropped off in front of St. Luke's for the first day of kindergarten. I watched, unable to comprehend why, in that moment when his mother tried to leave him at school, he was so terribly desperate to remain in her arms.

I know now that life, according to primary school, is all alphabetical, a world that cannot exist outside the confines of A to Z. At the onset of kindergarten, you become alphabetized, structured, and categorized according to your last name. The day can't begin until role is called, from Cole Adams to Sarah Zimmerman, one by one in a tedium of morning yawns. We were herded, from kindergarten through eighth grade, lined like a millipede from the church to the cafeteria, the cafeteria to the playground for recess, the playground back to the classroom.

The oppression of alphabetization meant that I was unable to know Julian well for the first few years of grade school. Sure, we ran and screamed and weaved our scrawny little bodies through playground equipment, racing down slides and throwing dirt clods at each other. But we were still strangers, unknowingly sequestered from the other half of ourselves. That was until we discovered each other at the age of ten, thanks to the fortuity of circumstance and common ground where the best of friendships can be fostered.

We played baseball as most American children do. Julian and I were fledgling boys, dressed by our mothers in uniforms too white to play in, swinging bats that were too heavy for our gangly arms. Neither of us having a father around for playing catch, we were by far the worst players on the team. That was why Coach Karr, a red-faced leprechaun of a man who was later banned from coaching for choking a twelve-year-old shortstop who didn't run out a grounder, sent the two of us into right and right center where we couldn't do as much damage. It was there in the outfield, separated by some forty green feet of manicured lawn, that we shared our first laugh as we played with dandelions and plucked handfuls of grass blades to toss into the wind. If I remember right, a fart joke was what first brought us together, a fart joke that was followed by juvenile, gut-busting guffaws over a word and a function that we have never stopped loving.

Throughout the season, the games took place almost without our knowing. Occasionally, a shot would be hit at us, and our mothers would scream and cheer encouragement as, shaken to attention, we ran down the ball and closed our eyes to throw it into the infield, praying it might hit somebody, anybody wearing a glove.

From what I have been told by my mother, despite Julian and I being a liability in the outfield and incessantly striking out or accidentally grounding out each time we got up to bat, the team went undefeated. And I remember, at the close of the season, there was a barbecue scheduled to follow a father and son game at the neighborhood diamond between Zephyr and Lyndover.

"You're not allowed to play," I told my mother when she came downstairs in her old high school softball uniform.

"Is your mother not good enough to play with the boys?"

"It's a father/son game," I protested.

"And you only have —" At that, she stopped. She had two greasy lines of eye black smeared across the tops of her cheeks and her ponytail pulled through the back of a mesh baseball cap, her uniform stretched tightly around her expanding form. On one hand, she wore her old mitt, and in the other, she held a casserole for the picnic, ready to fill both roles, to be my father and my mother on the same day. But in the end, she let me have my way.

Julian and I were dropped off separately by our mothers at the edge of the field, and we ran eagerly to join the game. The field was dusty, and the August sun was full and low and heat radiated off the pitcher's mound. The unfamiliar scent of aftershave that made me think of my uncles and grandfather followed Julian and me through the cluster of fathers paired with their sons to the front of the group, where we stood shoulder to shoulder and waited for Coach Karr to divvy us into teams.

It's possible that, before that afternoon, I just hadn't realized how it felt to be singled out, to be insignificant and inadequate because I didn't have a man standing behind me. But it was during that archaically cruel schoolyard picking of teams that I first truly felt incomplete, alone, and strangely isolated, as I watched the fathers grip the shoulders of their sons or ruffle the tops of their baseball caps.

Eventually, after the last father/son pairs were picked and the two of us were thrown onto a team, Coach Karr assigned us to our usual place in the right alcove of the outfield where we couldn't ruin the game, and we jogged out.

From the first at-bat, the lineup of the opposing team began to pick us apart, the fathers chipping balls at us, exposing the weakness of two boys who had never played a game of catch with their own dads. They did it out of cruelty and annoyance. There had to have been a dozen times when we had put a win in jeopardy, and the fathers were doing what fathers do. We tried our best, but as the game went on, we were battered and bruised by line drives and pop flies that we couldn't pull into our gloves. The game felt like it lasted the entire afternoon, and, to be honest, it probably had because Coach Karr was forced to keep coming out to check on Julian and me each time a ball careened off our shoulder or chest.

By the sixth inning, we were covered with welts, having faced more hits than we had all season. I kept dreaming of the moment when we could just eat hot dogs and drink Coca-Cola with the rest of the boys on our team. By the bottom of the sixth, the father playing left center, a blond man with broad shoulders who was growing tired of losing, pushed the two of us to the edge of the field by the chalked foul line where, I imagine, he hoped we couldn't sabotage the team anymore. It was then, on the very next at-bat, when a shot was clipped high into the air down the right-field line, that our baseball careers ended.

"Keep your glove up, Julian," Coach Karr hollered, his hoarse voice choking from the infield.

Julian stood under it and shuffled his feet, scurrying forward and backward as the ball sunk out of the sky toward him like a white asteroid. At the last second, the moment just before the ball fell into the webbing of his glove, he lost it in the sun and shifted his stance, and the ball cracked off his cheek with a smack. Julian fell to the ground, sobbing, his knees curled to his chest, face covered with his glove. Coach Karr, stretching up the belt of his baseball pants, spit, then started the long jog out to check on him for what must have been the tenth time that game. But Julian clearly had had enough. He stood up, stumbling and crying as he ran to the gap in the fence of the outfield and slipped through. I could hear them snickering, all the fathers and sons laughing, as I followed him away from the field.

"Julian," I called after him at the other side of Zephyr. He stopped and turned to me, sniffling as he wiped at his tears with the back of his baseball mitt. I simply nodded to him understandingly and then we continued on together in silence. We walked over to Sutton and turned north. By the time we reached his front yard, Julian had calmed down and his tears had dried.

"So, this is your house?" I said, turning to him. The top of his tanned cheek was red and welted and already splotched with the blue and purple of a black eye. I pointed in the direction of my house. "I live just over there. We're neighbors."

He smiled before heading to his front door. And from that moment on, we were inseparable.

CHAPTER 7

A RAINY DAY GAME

We followed the crowd east that Tuesday down the sidewalk of Clark Street in downtown St. Louis, walking shoulder to shoulder with other costumed fans toward the stadium. The two of us looked like boys, fully grown boys dressed up for a little league game in knit jerseys, our baseball caps pulled tightly down onto our heads. I wore home white, buttoned from my waist to the top of my chest, where it opened slightly, the stitched Cardinals logo covering the middle of my thin frame.

Like all games, I wore the number forty-five proudly. A number and a jersey make a statement, and it had taken some time to pick out. I remember first standing in the sporting goods store, my eyes jumping from one jersey to the next, name to name, number to number. There were home whites and away grays, specialty baby blue and red Dominican Republic, and breathable practice jerseys. So many options. As I stood there, I wondered what player I loved the most, but that led nowhere since I felt strongly about all of them, admiring each for different reasons. Albert Pujols, number five, with his Gold Glove Awards and strong bat seemed like the best choice. He was, at the time, hailed as the new king of swing, with the potential to be the greatest hitter and first baseman of all time.

But I struggled with the endless possibilities of trades and injuries and allegations. Remember, that was in the dark age of baseball, when every record and feat was scrutinized and marked with an asterisk, every hero checked for performance-enhancing drugs. There was HGH, which made athletes' heads swell like ripe watermelons. Then there were the injectables, countless anabolic steroids meant for doping racehorses. Every week it seemed a new player, some hero you'd never expect to be cheating, was exposed. Sometimes it was obvious, but more often than not you were left scratching your head, wondering if hair on the bottom of their feet or acne on their scalp were acceptable sacrifices. Was glory worth a deteriorated sperm count or a lifetime of malfunctioning erections? They risked everything, it seemed, just to be a little bit stronger. Players put their careers and lives in jeopardy to throw the ball just a little harder or swing a little faster. Many were subjected to congressional hearings and exposed as frauds, their legacies crushed by the twenty-four-hour sports networks with nothing better to cover. We had been living in the Steroid Era, as they called it, and standing in front of that wall of jerseys, I was reminded that heroes in the game of baseball rose and fell like families in America.

It was then, with the pockmarked teenaged store worker standing impatiently to my left in a referee's outfit with a plastic name tag pinned to his chest, that I saw the number forty-five, a number immortalized for every true Cardinals fan. The unparalleled Bob Gibson, one of the greatest pitchers of all time, seemed right. I had wanted something strong and lasting, after all.

I thought of what I had once read of Gibson, a quote from Hank Aaron. Supposedly, the home run king had told a young rookie who was getting ready to face Gibson that you "don't dig in against Bob Gibson; he'll knock you down. He'd knock down his own grandmother if she dared to challenge him. Don't stare at him, don't smile at him, don't talk to him. He doesn't like it. If you happen to hit a home run, don't run too slow, don't run too fast. If you want to celebrate, get in the tunnel first. And if he hits you, don't charge the mound because he's a Golden Gloves boxer." The number forty-five was perfect.

From then on, I wore the number proudly to every game I attended, and even sometimes at home while I watched on television. I began collecting number forty-fives, going so far as to drop nearly seven hundred dollars on one at an auction. It was an authentic, autographed jersey, which I framed to hang in my living room above the fireplace like a family portrait.

However, it was the original, the first Bob Gibson jersey that I ever bought, the home white, that I wore on that Tuesday afternoon as I walked shoulder to shoulder with Julian. I remember Julian was wearing an authentic but anonymous and numberless away jersey. He hadn't put nearly as much thought into his jersey choice. For him, it wasn't about homage or fandom. Rather, he chose the away jersey because he knew he looked good in gray.

It was rare for a weekday game, especially one in June—only the second month of a long season—to be sold out, but that Tuesday afternoon was special, and the streets were a lovely moving pastiche of red and white and gray. The Chicago Cubs were in town, and all of St. Louis turned out. St. Louis loved their Cardinals and hated the Cubs more than any other team in the Major League, cherishing the years of loathing that brewed in the National League Central, where each year they contended for one of the precious few playoff spots.

It was more than a rivalry because rivalries come and go. A rivalry can ease and pass as events unfold. Tense pennant chases and dugout-clearing brawls bring them on, boiling the blood of fans. But as quickly as a rivalry can rise, it will fade because of a few years of yawn-inducing performances. If one half of the rivalry slumps, everyone stops paying attention and forgets who they hated and why.

The Cubs and Cardinals were not rivals. What they had—or at least their fans had—was a hatred, a feud that had lasted for over a century. Rivalries and competition may very well have been why God and man created sports, but it is the hatred that sells out stadiums. Each of the one hundred and sixty-two games counted, and if you were a true fan, you followed each game and the scores of everyone else in the NLC. Julian and I, like good and loyal Cardinals fans, would check the scores of all the teams in the division daily. If the Cardinals won, we celebrated. If the Cubs lost, we celebrated even more.

A feud like the one between the Cubs and Cardinals would sell out Wrigley Field and Busch Stadium whenever they met. It didn't matter if it was a rainy weekday game when both teams were far out of contention. In St. Louis, people would do whatever they had to just to make it to the game, whether it meant finding a babysitter or calling in sick to work.

Julian and I had taken off an afternoon of work for just such a game. It was a Tuesday with gray skies, and both teams were already below five hundred as they dragged the bottom rungs of the division.

"It look like rain to you?"

We continued on with the tide of fans to the edge of the street. A police officer with a bristled mustache guided traffic, blowing his whistle and waving his hands at the cars and people. At the curb, we were motioned to a halt along with the rest of the crowd.

There was a warm weight to the air, and the entire dull sky was filled with clouds that were settling lower and lower as they promised to burst and wash all the dust and dirt off the city.

"I didn't check the forecast, but it doesn't look good," I said.

"We're going to get pissed on," Julian said as we waited for the light to change.

I looked up at the towering red brick of Busch Stadium across the street as it filled steadily with fans.

When the light changed, we crossed, waved along by the traffic officer in his reflective yellow vest. At the corner of Clark and 7th, we fell under the shadow of the massive stadium. The sidewalk was adorned with statues of all of our heroes. This was hallowed ground. Each figure stood only a few feet tall, forged of bronze and cast in stances and poses individual to what they brought to the great game of baseball. Ozzie Smith was eternally diving forward, making one of those acrobatic catches that helped define a Hall of Fame career and earn him the nickname "The Wizard." Slaughter was there too, along with Brock and many others. I looked between and through the crowd for Bob Gibson. I had stopped to admire his statue at least a hundred times. He was cast in that famous follow-through of his, nearly parallel to the ground because he'd throw every pitch so hard that he'd almost fall over. But the sea of jerseys and caps—red and white and gray, with the occasional splotch of blue—was too dense to see through.

The noise from the stadium was growing, the hollers and conversations and pregame cheers and jeers all mixed together into a rumble. I waited, aching for it to explode into a deafening roar of exaltations or condemnations. A flock of birds, sparrows or blackbirds I supposed, flew away from their nests and perches hidden somewhere in the impossibly high nooks and crannies of the infinite red bricks of Busch Stadium.

At Spruce, we hung a left, along with the crowd, only to be stifled by the clogged line waiting to have their tickets taken at the third-base entrance. Everyone shuffled forward, inch by inch, one by one, as they passed through the turnstiles. Julian looked up, examining the massive bronze statue of Stan Musial that stared down an imaginary pitcher. He had seen the statue a thousand times, the first being when his mother had taken him to a game as a young boy and let him climb on its base with all the other kids. Stan "the Man" was still a hero to Julian, the baseball equivalent of Superman, even though he had been born too late to see Musial play an inning or take a single swing. Julian had been told, when he was just three, that Stan Musial was the greatest Cardinal, possibly even the greatest ballplayer, who had ever lived and that he deserved the statue that stood twice the height of any man.

Making our way past the turnstile, we pushed through the throng to find our seats, which were only a few rows back from the dugout, where we nestled in with our Big Gulp–sized plastic cups of Bud Light. The field was so close, the players so real on the perfectly manicured grass. There was almost too much to take in, what, with the expanse of the field and the size of the stadium, a soup bowl for the gods underneath the wide-open summer sky.

Once the players of both clubs had finished with batting practice, the grounds crew prepped the field. I looked to the giant television above the outfield bleachers that was big enough to have its own piece of the skyline and studied the stats of each player as they flashed unnaturally bright on the screen.

"Bud! Ice-cold Bud Light!" a hunched and weathered vendor called out to all the fans as he descended the stairs of our section, stopping every few rows to set down his tub and pour a beer. He made his living that way, just like the hot dog, cotton candy, and peanut vendors, all of them hiking mountains of stairs, carrying their bins and change purses to serve everyone enjoying the game. Since we were boys, Julian and I had always said that vendors had the greatest job in the whole world because they were paid to watch the games day in and out.

After the injuries and scratches were announced over the PA system, we rose to our feet and ceremoniously removed our hats before holding them over our hearts for the national anthem, which was belted out by a portly diva whose high-pitched, long-winded notes extended each and every word, pushing each high and low to the limits of the scale with an infusion of soul. Her warbling made the whole thing last entirely too long. Children stirred and adults yawned or shuffled their feet. Even the Marine Color Guard had let the flag dip.

We ordered two more beers and a bag of peanuts when the game started. Inning by inning, hit by hit, and run by run, we watched and cheered. Julian and I kept up with our tradition of ordering a fresh beer at the top of each inning. By the top of the fourth, I could see the rain falling off in the distance. Then the skyline above the city burst, the winds increasing and casting sheets of rain onto the scrambling crowd of fans in the centerfield bleachers as the silver Gateway Arch, the elbow of some Grecian god's coat hanger, half-buried just above the muddied banks of the Mississippi, grew dark and wet.

The air was still warm, smelling of fresh-cut grass and baseball. I continued to watch the crowd beyond the outfield wall panic as the thunderstorm dumped on them. Julian and I laughed aloud at the fans stumbling out of their seats and covering their heads as they scrambled up the aisles. Then, before I could react, it was on us too, the fat droplets pounding down, weighing down our jerseys and khaki shorts. I cupped my hand over the top of my beer and shoved Julian to the concrete stairs of the aisle, and we hustled up along with everyone else to the safety of the high-arching brick ceilings that covered the concourse. At the top of the stairs, we huddled together with the crowd of wet dogs and hoped to ride out the storm in the long washroom and concession lines. Down on the field, a dozen boys dragged a gargantuan tarp behind them and covered the infield. The rain was coating the stands, soaking the game, and threatening to ruin our entire day.

"What's the word?" I asked the moment I returned from the urinal troughs to find Julian leaning against a condiment stand, holding a cup of beer dripping with rainwater in one hand and playing with his phone in the other.

"It hasn't slowed down yet," he said without looking up. "I overheard some guys who said it isn't supposed to stop all afternoon."

Fans in wet red and gray meandered all around us, their voices combining and bouncing off the walls so that I had to shout in order for Julian to hear me. Everything felt damp, and I was starting to get cold.

"You want to hang out until they call it? Or head somewhere else?"

"Up to you," he said, tipping up the last of his beer.

"I don't feel like waiting around here all day just to have them call the game."

"Yeah," he agreed, dropping his cup to the floor where the plastic rattle was lost in the din of the crowd. "Let's go to the Landing and get something to eat."

My jersey was sticking to my skin, bunching as I followed Julian sideways through the crowd of people out the turnstiles of the stadium. At the corner of 7th and Spruce, we flagged down a taxi in the rain.

"The Landing," I told the driver as we crawled inside. The downpour rattled on the roof as we took off, chilling in the air conditioning of the taxi, soaked through to the bone. I felt hungry and considered the options that awaited us at the Landing, that infamous bar and restaurant district on the waterfront of the Mississippi. Throughout the day, the cobblestone streets were packed with people meeting for lunch in the restaurants that transformed into dank bars and sweaty dance clubs once it got late enough.

The driver, a lumpy man dressed too warmly for the season, headed around the stadium on Plaza, then headed east on Walnut. At Memorial, he turned north. The streets were congested, dripping, and sopping, the oil slicks shimmering in the headlights of the streaming cars that weaved in and out of each other in a rhythm that almost seemed designed and purposeful.

Before I knew it, we were underneath the Eads Bridge, the game behind us and almost forgotten. The MetroLink rumbled overhead as we took Washington toward the river, then turned onto 1st.

"This is good," Julian said to the driver at Morgan Street. He paid, and we got out and ran to the shelter of an awning across the street from a parking garage.

"Where to? I'm starving," he said as he took off his baseball cap and slicked back the wet hair from his face with his fingertips.

"How about the Drunken Fish?"

"No sushi. I'm already wet. I don't need women thinking I'm a fucking fisherman fresh from the wharf."

I laughed. "Joey B's?"

"I had pizza for dinner last night."

"Skybox?"

"I didn't know we were still twenty-one," he mocked.

I knew this game. Julian's faux indecisiveness was one of his little manipulation techniques that assured he got his way in the end. He would let you make suggestions, sometimes a seemingly countless stream of proffers, until he finally threw out one of his own, the one he knew he'd wanted all along. Julian's first suggestion was always the deciding factor on where to go or what to do or eat after he had let you feel like you were part of the decision-making process. It was a game of attrition, really.

I played along. Hannegan's? No, he wasn't in the mood. Jake's? No, we were underdressed. Tigin's? No, too Irish. Buffet on the Admiral Casino? This last one was a joke, and he didn't even bother to respond.

"How about the Feisty Bulldog?" he finally suggested, breaking the stalemate.

"Sounds good to me."

The Bulldog was on 1st and Lucas, some two blocks away, so we hoofed it across the ancient cobblestone streets and empty sidewalks. True to form, the rain gave up no sooner than we walked through the door and asked for a table.

The hostess led us through the late lunch crowd and the afternoon drinkers getting an early start. We sat at a booth and ordered burgers and beers, then ate and watched the highlights of baseball games from around the country on the flat screens hung on walls next to neon signs.

An English pub of sorts, the Bulldog had international flags and soccer décor hanging from every available inch of the walls and ceiling. The light was dim and artificial, the ambient noise a chaos of slurs and laughter. Everything smelled like stale beer and urine, and the whole place was one giant room built only of wood. From the slats of polished flooring to the booths and tables built on top of them, it was all wood. The ceiling was high, maybe twenty feet above us, and the walls holding it up were as timber as all the rest. I felt like we were inside some elephantine redwood in the mists of the Pacific Northwest where a madman had carved out a windowless bar that towered high above the canopy of the forest.

Julian ordered more beers, pints of Schlafly Pale this time. I was stuffed, bloated, so I unbuckled to let my stomach breathe. I belched, then talked to Julian about work. The server cleared away our plates and empty glasses, and we ordered another round, then another. I tried, then, to get drunk, but it wasn't working. I had eaten too much, and each sip was a struggle, as if taking in any more would pop my innie to an outie.

By the time the sun set out there somewhere left of the city, I was feeling lightheaded, tired, and tossed around. Julian was standing by the bar and talking to a woman a few years younger than us. He wore a look of triumph on his face and winked at me as he raised still another sweating glass to his lips. I tilted my head to get a good look at the woman. She looked to be another rained-out Cardinals fan who wore a pair of high-cut white shorts that compounded the illusion that her lovely legs were as slender and long as a mannequin's in a store window. Her flaxen hair flowed from beneath a baseball cap and fell down around her shoulders. I stared at her legs, fully aware of how low my eyes must have looked as I slouched in the booth, my right half facing the bar while my left was angled toward the gorgeous underaged hostesses and the front door.

I hadn't seen our server in a while, so I decided to stretch my legs. I got up with a groan and headed over to the bar a few stools down from Julian and waited for a drink. Julian took off his cap and slipped his fingers through his black hair.

"Oh, I love your hair," I heard the woman say to Julian. I watched as she reached up and played with it, stroking the side of his face with her hand.

"Thanks," he said with a cocky smile. "I grow it myself."

When she giggled, as though he had said something clever, Julian began caressing her hip while I tried my best not to laugh.

My drink came just in time because I had to piss again, so I backed away from the bar and somehow managed to bump into another customer, a rail of a man with gangly arms.

"Watch where you're fucking going!"

"Sorry." I staggered backward.

"You should be," he said, and poked me in the chest with an outstretched finger that reminded me of Spielberg's E.T.

"Calm down," I suggested.

"Who the fuck are you telling to calm down?"

All the conversations around us cut out, and as the hush settled over the bar, I was reminded of those old spaghetti westerns. I found myself staring at the man's chest as he stepped closer still. His blue shirt was adorned with a capital C and a bear whelp. Gritting my teeth a bit, I feigned something like anger in an attempt to look as if I were truly offended by this alien fan insulting me in my own city. I even tapped my knuckles against the side of my leg, knowing deep down that the only thing I honestly felt in that moment was the overwhelming need to use the restroom.

"You hear me?" he demanded, and I saw the scar, the deep cleft on his lip that he probably hadn't been born with. It was the sort of scar that had been given to him as an unwanted gift. I knew then he was more than a Cubs fan. He was a lifelong fan. A hopeful. An asshole.

You see, the Cubs had always been a disappointment, perennial failures for more than a century. The name of their greatest demigod, the late and great Harry Caray, said it all. He was their announcer, taken in as the voice of the Cubs after he was fired by KMOX in St. Louis. He recorded a version of the song "Take Me Out to the Ball Game" and was loved by his listeners for his undying loyalty to the perpetually floundering Cubs. Like I said, though, his name said it all. To be a lifelong Cubs fan meant committing to the feudal samurai hara-kiri year after year. Hara-kiri. Harry Caray. The sound is identical. At the devastating and disappointing conclusion of each season, you want nothing more than to slip a tanto short sword into the side of your abdomen and slide it across, spilling your guts. Seppuku was the only thing any lifelong Cubs fan had to look forward to. Hopeless hope and hara-kiri season after season.

Cubs fans did the same thing every year with the hope of a different outcome. It's the very definition of insanity. And even though all Cardinal-loving people everywhere hated the Cubs, we still felt sorry for them. While we had won championships, enjoyed dynasties of success, they'd floundered, squandering chance after chance, year after year. They were cursed, black goat and all, and to embrace such a thing, to be a fan of a star-crossed, luckless franchise, meant a lifetime of disappointment and sorrow. This man who stood before me at the Bulldog lived that bedeviled, though insanely hopeful, existence, and that made him dangerous.

"Sorry," I conceded, looking down to my feet. "I'll watch where I'm going next time."

He murmured something and let me pass. My hand was shaking, and I had forgotten where I was going until the sting returned, so I rushed to the restroom.

"You really showed that guy," Julian said when I met him back at our booth, his eyes red with tears from laughing at me.

I slid in across from him and felt like slapping the grin off his face. It was strange, but I wanted to hit him more than I had the man who'd threatened me.

"Where the hell were you?"

"Talking to that girl." He pointed with an outstretched pint in his fingertips.

"Oh, yeah. Did you get her number?"

He smiled that coy Julian smile. I hated it.

"Well, fucking bravo to you," I said, then waved for our server's attention.

"What's your problem?"

"You don't have to laugh at me, Julian."

"Oh, come on." He pointed to his half-empty pint, then held up two fingers to the server. "Who can you laugh at if you can't laugh at yourself? And who would you rather have laugh at you than your best friend?"

I tore at a paper napkin with my fingers. It was dark out, and I couldn't see through the front windows of the restaurant to the street.

"What happened anyway?"

"I don't know," I said. "He was just some asshole Cubs fan."

"Well, from the looks of it, you forgot to bring your balls to the fight."

"What fight?"

"The one that would have happened if you had remembered to bring your balls." He laughed as only a prick would.

"What was I supposed to do?"

"Hell, I don't know. You work out, don't you?" He paused while the server placed two more beers that tasted like Pabst in front of us. "You should have fought him."

"In the bar?"

"Sure, I guess."

"I've never been in a fight," I admitted.

"Neither have I." He took a sip. "He wasn't very big though."

I wasn't quite sure what to say. The subject had never really come up in all our years of knowing each other. Neither of us had been in a fight, nor had we really even been confronted, except in the seventh grade when Peter Crass had shoved Julian during a basketball game at recess. I remember Julian fell back, turning into the winged blades of my shoulder for a fat lip. He left the court crying, convinced we had jarred one of his bottom teeth loose.

"Is that what men are supposed to do?"

"What?" Julian asked.

"Fight," I said. "Is that what men like us are supposed to do? Are we supposed to defend our honor and kick the shit out of everyone who crosses us?"

We both sat silent. Julian looked to the cobwebbed lighting that hung from the ceiling. I was growing sleepier by the minute and looked at my watch. The afternoon of drinking had started some six hours before, and I was hearing the call of my goose-down comforter and the softness of my sheets.

"Oh my God." My body tensed as panic ripped through me. I jolted upright and looked past Julian's shoulder to the opened front door of the Feisty Bulldog.

"What is it?" Julian asked.

"She's here."

"You're fucking joking," he said, sinking deep into the booth. "She" required no explanation.

Feeling much like I imagine a deer does in the headlights of an oncoming car, I stared back at her now-rounded face. We had let our guard down, made ourselves vulnerable, and now here was Maria, standing in the doorway of the bar with her hands on her hips, her back arched to support the doming egg of her pregnant belly.

"You knew this was coming," I whispered over the table as I hunched forward, trying in vain to break her line of sight and hide.

Julian ducked lower into the booth, shaking his head.

"Just talk to her. Tell her you were scared or something." This seemed to make sense, though I wasn't sure I could ever imagine how angry a woman, abandoned and pregnant, could be. "You can't run forever."

"Get down, you asshole," Julian snapped, but Maria could already sense him, like a bloodhound on the trail of an escaped convict. She started over, waddling on the hardwood floor with wide, Humpty Dumpty steps.

"It's too late," I said, feeling the hairs on the back of my neck stand up and scream.

"Fuck it," Julian said as he squirmed out of the booth. And then, once his feet hit the floor, he was off, darting through the bar with a speed only those in life-threatening situations were rumored to possess.

Maria had seen him and was in hot pursuit, moving as quickly as a woman could at six months pregnant. I knew I had to run too, but I wasn't sure if I was up for it. I was getting tired.

Then I heard the fire alarm door screech and wail, and I knew he was free, narrowly escaping out into the open where she couldn't possibly catch up. The alarm meant he had made it through the back door and out into the alleyway where he could run and hide in the fog and darkness of the river bottom night.

CHAPTER 8

September 5, 1998

We were fourteen when I invited Bethany Hilliard over on a Tuesday afternoon in July. My mother was working, which meant we had the house to ourselves. It had been a month since Julian had lost his virginity, and I'd decided that if he was ready, I was too.

I had heard stories about Beth and knew that she liked me. We had talked on the phone, and she had told me her bra size and all the things she had done with other boys, and I had jacked off while I listened to her, breathing away from the receiver so she couldn't tell what I was doing. On that Tuesday, we kissed and fondled each other on the living room couch, then she took me in her hand, refusing to use her mouth, which, in hindsight, I'm incredibly grateful for considering the face full of metal braces she had at the time. I pushed my hand down her pants, feeling the softness of her curled pubic hairs and touching the warmth of her.

"Do you want to?" I asked her. Halfway through her nod, I pulled off her shorts and panties like a magician ripping away the curtain for the grand reveal, then tossed them over my shoulder. She smelled like suntan lotion and her breasts were large, the areolas perfectly rounded like two petite pancakes. I'm not sure I had seen breasts that large before, and for a moment I thought of my mother.

"You better be careful with girls like that," my mother had said to me when she caught me ogling the cans of a swimsuit model on the E! channel. "Tits like that will go straight to your ass once you get older. They'll sag too. Young girls with big breasts always end up fat when they get older."

"Come on, Mom," was all I could do to respond. "I don't want to hear stuff like that from you."

"I'm just warning you," she had said. "Marry a girl like that and you will end up staring at a huge ass for the rest of your life."

Who the hell could think about marriage? I just wanted to have them in my face, in my hands.

I pinched Bethany's nipples between my finger and thumb, working them like a safecracker as I kissed her and felt her begin to tremble. I knew she was thinking about it, considering me as her first.

"What about your mother?" she said. "It's almost four."

My mother wouldn't be home for another hour, maybe two. There was plenty of time. But suddenly, I felt sick to my stomach. And I realized then that it wasn't getting caught that terrified me. Rather, it had all become so real, so possible. And I became scared to death of this girl, of being inside of her and losing my virginity.

"You're right," I lied, masking my cowardice with what I thought was a suave intonation. I told her we didn't want to be interrupted, speaking to her as if I was some sort of expert lover who could go on for hours.

She may have been disappointed, but she still smiled and then kissed me in a sweet, wet way that made me feel absolved. We dressed and watched television and then she slipped out the back of the house when we heard the garage door opening and my mother calling out, "Honey, I'm home," like Desi Arnaz, which, incidentally, made me Lucille Ball.

I told Julian all about it. I told him how Bethany looked naked, and how she smelled. He said she was fat, and I hated him for that. Then I lied. I lied to my best friend because men are supposed to want sex—we aren't supposed to be afraid. I told him how she had ridden me and even produced a condom that I had soiled for the occasion.

I didn't actively pursue sex again for the next few years, though I claimed to. Julian and I would have conquests, though I developed a convenient "gentlemen never tell" motto that allowed me to only gloss over the sex I wasn't having.

To be perfectly honest, I was still terrified when it finally did happen. It was my first semester at SLU, and I was living in Griesedieck, a sixteen-story high-rise dormitory conjoined on either side by two squat buildings, Walsh and Clemens Halls. Together, the three looked like a giant cock and balls. We lovingly called it "the Dick" or "Greasy Dick" or "Shaft."

Her name was Brynn Ratcliff, a sophomore communications major with blonde highlights in her straight hair. She was a Zeta Tau Alpha who wore nothing but pink and teal, always pairing a sorority-branded t-shirt with an endless rotation of jean skirts and shorts. We met at Humphrey's, the campus bar on the corner of Laclede and Spring. It was warm outside, and she approached me as I waited to the left of the drink well, working as hard as I could to get drunk. She asked me about my major and the other blasé and stock topics that college kids talk about. I brushed my leg against hers, admiring her perfectly polished toes. Strawberry daiquiri was what she called it.

We sat in a booth, talking and drinking for the next few hours. She smoked while she stroked my leg through my olive-colored corduroy pants, from my knee to the uppermost part of my thigh. We kissed right there in the bar, in a sea of some hundred or so drunk students smoking and talking loudly. Her eyes looked heavy, and I imagine mine did as well.

Within an hour, we were back in my room in towering Griesedieck, where I had been randomly paired with a homesick roommate to whom I barely spoke. The dorm room was cramped with two beds lofted high above the tiled floor, and the light from the city lit our bodies up with a blue haze void of any definitive detail. Before I could explain myself to Brynn, my pants were off, a pile of olive on the floor, and she had taken off her shirt and hiked up her skirt. She held the tip of the condom and rolled the rest down onto me, then hopped on. There wasn't time to be worried, to be scared the way I was with Bethany. I was on bottom throughout, making faces that I imagine ranged anywhere from ecstasy to terror.

We went home together night after night during the weeks that followed, tangling together in drunken, rabid sexual ferocity. We drank and then screwed, nothing more, nothing less. I never told her about my virginity, opting instead to just get better with the experience she was generously providing. I made mistakes, of course. Mis-stabbings and pinchings. But eventually, I learned. I learned what to do to women, in addition to all the personal joys and pleasures I had been missing due to fear. However, I learned nothing of Brynn beyond the contours, smells, and tastes of her young body.

And then, as quickly as it had begun, things with Brynn ended when I met someone else, another girl. I'm not sure why this is the case, but college makes it all too easy. I wanted to taste every flavor that these girls had to offer, and whenever words like relationship or dating cropped up, I became ornery and fled. The other men, boys really, were doing the same, and we shared stories about who had slept with whom, who was good at this and that. Things Julian had been talking about for years. It didn't make any sense to call these girls sluts, but we still did. When men are promiscuous, it's celebrated. Even as a boy, I could see the illogic of these skewed sexual norms and nomenclatures, but I could never think of a way to change it or even a reason why I would. Why shake the foundations of a system that works so unflinchingly in your favor?

CHAPTER 9

BETTER LYING THROUGH ADVERTISING

I walked into Belzer and Bauman's Advertising, Inc. at a quarter to nine the morning after Julian and I had abruptly parted ways when Maria had spoiled our night at the Feisty Bulldog. I had sunk as low as possible into the booth when she paused, looked me dead in the eye, and said "Don't fucking move!" before pursuing Julian through the whining fire exit and into the back alley behind the restaurant. The moment she was out of sight, I had tossed a few too many twenties onto the table and made a run for it out the front door.

As I made my way through the lower-ranking cubicles toward my corner office, I tried to push Julian and Maria from my mind in an effort to focus on the day before me.

Advertising was never something I had aspired to do, but I had a talent for it and had become successful. It all started when my mother had demanded I get myself a job or an internship one afternoon in my junior year of college when I had brought home the gift of thirty pounds of dirty laundry. I didn't argue because I had counted myself lucky to have gotten by doing so little for so long, though I certainly didn't run out and take a job waiting tables or tending bar either. I explained to her that such menial work wasn't an option for me and instead sought out the right fit for someone of my talents and demeanor.

Then, after nearly a full semester of dragging my feet, I noticed the flyer for an internship at Belzer and Bauman and decided that a desk job at an advertising agency would both appease my mother and afford me the freedom to do what I wanted. In the end, the interview process didn't seem to amount to much, and I was given the internship. I learned later—much later—that my mother had convinced her father to pull some strings.

For the next two years, between running errands and getting coffee, I bided my time at B and B by hiding in my little cubicle and pretending to work, planning to quit the moment I graduated. That is until I was offered a full-time job assisting one of the senior copywriters and decided to abandon all the artistic integrity I had once held so dearly.

You see, my aversion to such an opportunity had once stemmed from the illusion that I was an artist. Throughout college, I had wanted and pretended to be a writer. I took creative writing and literature classes and daydreamed about one day living like the old expatriates. I wanted to be Hemingway or Fitzgerald, writing and drinking myself into a stupor in Parisian cafes, sharing stories and gossiping with other artists, summering in the South of France, and making love to all the beautiful women I could get my hands on.

However, I never wrote more than a few short stories, mostly biographical stuff that my teachers felt was profound and showed promise as long as I was willing to take the time to revise. I wasn't. In fact, most of my short-lived writing career, during the time I majored in English at SLU, had been idled away in campus bars and parties. I spent far more time talking about writing than actually writing and used being a soulful, aspiring novelist to meet and sleep with girls, which actually worked quite well. For a time, I had no more plans than to graduate and save money while I holed myself up in my mother's basement to compose my masterpiece. But, as May and graduation grew closer, the internship, the position I had applied for on a whim and had gotten because of my mother, soon evolved into an offer I never expected to get.

One day, as I was preparing to leave early for lunch, two of the senior partners of Belzer and Bauman stopped by my cubicle to invite me in for a closed-door meeting. I followed them into a glass conference room, and they asked me to have a seat at the end of a long table. I was wearing an off-brand dress shirt and black pants that hadn't been truly black for some time. The partners were old, with liver spots and tired suits, crowns in their fake smiles and bad breath.

One of them told me that, during my time at the firm, I had impressed a number of people, although to this day I have no idea how. They felt I had promise and slid a piece of paper across to me. I nearly refused to turn it over, recognizing this as my crossroads, the moment at which I had to choose artistic integrity (real or imagined) over career and bourgeoisie success. But curiosity got the best of me, and as I turned over that piece of clean paper, I was given a glimpse of all I could have. The figure they offered provided just a taste of what could be made, the zeros on the end of that entry-level salary sparking a greedy hunger in me that I hadn't known existed. I had never imagined I could be worth that much, so I of course accepted their offer on the spot, forgetting my supposed artistic integrity. And for that money, like a loyal little labrador, I spent the better part of my twenties under Raleigh Metzler.

Raleigh was an inept copywriter with archaic ideas, dusty suits, and an unforgivable mustache that looked, when he spoke too closely to you, as though it had sprouted from somewhere deep inside his cavernous nostrils. He would have retired, I learned after a few months as his assistant, but he had gambled and divorced his way out of nearly every penny he had ever earned. Despite his incompetence, the partners at the firm didn't have the heart to lay him off because he had been there for more than thirty years. So they played the waiting game.

I grew used to accepting my place as the hidden source of his ideas. Every proposal or project he was praised for was an unsaid pat on the back for me, something I would eventually be rewarded for. And then, after five long years, it was all handed to me on a silver platter when old Raleigh collapsed from heart failure as he was running to catch a bus. A salary like that, and he still rode the bus to work.

Within a week, I had moved into Raleigh's office, a fish tank of glass windows that ran the length of the room from floor to ceiling. I walked in every day to sit in my plush leather chair to work at my mahogany desk, my back facing the light pouring in from Locust Street.

"Any messages?" I asked Alicia, my secretary, who, according to an ethics and office decorum seminar, I had to call an "administrative assistant."

She was in her mid-twenties, a brunette with strong thighs. We had slept together once after an office Christmas party and never spoke of it. She had a son, a five-year-old, and was intelligent and beautiful, and I felt that life had dealt her one of the most rotten hands possible: knocked up in college by some deadbeat, an event that had led to her dropping out and taking a job as a secretary and cementing her life as a second-class citizen. The night we slept together was special, but only in the sense that I could tell it had nothing to do with a raise. She genuinely wanted me and afterward was ashamed for having a life I couldn't share with her.

"Just what you have there on your desk," Alicia said at my door. "Can I get you anything, Mr. Corwin?" She had only called me Brett on the one occasion when we were at our most intimate.

"Nothing right now."

She nodded and started away.

"That outfit looks fantastic." I leaned back in my chair and wasn't lying. She wore a pencil skirt and heels, and the top of her frilly yet professional white blouse was open. "Is it new?"

She smiled and said yes.

"I love it," I said, and with a turn in my high-backed desk chair and a shuffle of the papers on my desk, she knew it was time to leave.

For the next hour or so, I caught up on emails and memos, putting off a phone call until closer to lunch when there wasn't much of a chance to reach the client. It wasn't that I was lazy or that I wasn't excited about the work. To be honest, I just didn't have any ideas. I had been handed the assignment of an Omaha-based company called E-First, which hoped to bring ethanol fuels to the world stage by creating a multisource advertising campaign that included web penetration.

Web-based advertising was my specialty as one of the few non-archaic copywriters at Belzer and Bauman. It became my division of sorts, my focus. Raleigh hadn't been the only person at B and B who was behind the times. It was an old company, one surviving since before the First World War, which was something that companies looking to advertise relished, but it also meant that the majority of people working there were relics, dinosaurs who never got over the Madison Avenue "man's man's" world of the fifties—whatever the hell that actually meant. I was the resident expert on the internet simply because I was the only senior member of Belzer and Bauman born after the Carter administration.

When I started my internship, advertising meant nothing more to me than entertaining commercials and an avenue to release some creativity upon the world without tapping into any of the good stuff. I thought I was a writer, and there wasn't much out there that pays for the food of a creative mind. And on that day when I had seen all the numbers on that salary offer, the artistically creative side of me died. I saved no ideas and wrote no more. My life became about what I could afford, the places I could eat, and the clothes I could wear, and I tried to keep up with Julian's habits. My condo was one step below his townhouse, but I dressed just as smartly.

At noon, I picked up the phone, confident that the people in Omaha were taking their lunch, gobbling up Reubens with a side of deep-fried mayonnaise or whatever it was they ate there. I dialed Clark, the marketing manager for E-First. I was counting on him being out since I had nothing to tell him.

"Hello." His secretary—administrative assistant, whatever—had a soft, sweet voice. She spoke with the coy innocence of a former cheerleader given the job for her legs.

"Hi there, sweetheart. This is Brett Corwin over here at Belzer and Bauman in Missouri. Is Clark in?"

"Mr. Clark has been expecting your call," she said, and then I realized that Clark was his last name, not his first, so now my art designer owed me lunch. "I'll put you right through."

Shit!

"Brett." The voice was guttural, and I imagined an old fellow with suspenders stretched to their breaking point, the elastic trying desperately to hold back the tide of his man breasts. "How the hell are you?"

"Oh, great, great," I tried to recover, conscious of the choking surprise in my voice. "How is everything over there in Omaha?"

I had never been there and was trying to picture where the city was on a map. Was it the capital of Nebraska? No, that's Lincoln. I imagined it somewhere by Wyoming and Kansas at the same time.

"Damn hot," he said. I could hear his chair creak loudly, and I pictured his bulk relaxing back into it. His voice was low and friendly—there was no hint of nasal or twang in his words. He sounded neither Southern nor Northern, and I couldn't place the accent. There was something wholly American and goodhearted to his dialect, yet it was empty and seemingly disingenuous. His voice was generic, sounding as if he was from nowhere.

"Well, I hope you're keeping cool somehow." I tried to force a laugh, but it didn't go well, and I needed to shift gears. "I just thought I would touch base with you on this web campaign."

I glanced up from my desk. The blinds of my glass front wall were open, and I watched Julian as he walked toward my office. Alicia stood up quickly from her desk, and he smiled at her but refused to stop. I covered the receiver of the telephone, still listening to Clark's ramblings about the weather and God knows what else. Julian threw open my office door and slid into the room with a kick to his left and a grandiose spin. He was dressed fashionably lazy in khakis, a soft gray t-shirt, and a pair of deck shoes. His black hair was tossed back, carelessly pushed behind his ears.

Mr. Clark was still talking. "I just went over the outline proofs you sent over."

"Mm-hmm." I nodded to Alicia, who was standing in the doorway with a look of concern. She had met Julian a few times before—days when he had surprised me. It was always random and unnecessary, and I got the impression that she didn't care for him. "I understand." I had no idea what I was agreeing with as I watched Alicia back out and click the door shut.

Julian wandered around my office, poking at the Ficus in the corner, then walking over to examine the Coca-Cola ad from the 19th century I had hanging on my wall. Like a child, he poked at a portrait of a posh Victorian girl, dressed to the gills with lace and frills, sitting in front of a silver tea set and looking more like a doll than anything that moved or breathed.

"Is this real?" Julian poked the painting.

"Yes." I covered the receiver tightly. "Sit the fuck down. This is important."

Julian danced to some imaginary music, then plopped down into the chair and crossed his legs.

Mr. Clark said something else.

"Well, we can take the campaign in a different direction if you like," I pandered.

"I'm just not sure you appreciate what we're doing over here." He was being short with me, and although I was tempted to interrupt, I didn't. "E-First is tackling the agricultural surplus while providing an environmentally friendly fuel. I hired you and your company to take us to the next level. We took a lot of heat by not keeping this job in Omaha and, in looking at these proofs, I'm worried we shouldn't have trusted your reputation."

"You were right to trust it." I instantly felt aggressive, cornered. "If anyone can help E-First achieve success, it is Belzer and Bauman. If you just tell me what you want, what is wrong with the proofs and the concept, then I can make it right."

He let the words drift in the air for a while.

"I'm not sure it's that simple," he muttered.

Julian realized I was in trouble. He sat back and relaxed, the corner of his mouth turned in a subtle smile, so he could enjoy watching me squirm.

"I'm thinking the problem might be a lack of familiarity," Clark said.

"I understand." I couldn't, for the life of me, remember what the hell I had sent him and was trying desperately to pull it up on my computer. I juggled dozens of clients, most of whom simply told me what they wanted, then I did it. This was a new company who had no idea how advertising worked. I should have been babying them, but I just couldn't find the time to care.

"I'm thinking that the only way for you to best represent us is for you to really get an idea of what we do."

"Of course," I said.

Julian stared at me, bored now. I expected him to start dancing or making faces for attention at any moment.

"You need to see the operation firsthand."

"See what?"

"These ethanol plants," Clark spoke quickly. "They are a sight to see."

"In Nebraska?"

"Where else? Once you see them, and you really get a handle on what we're doing out here, then I think you will be able to truly represent us."

"I'm not sure this time of year —"

"These plants—well, they're like cities, really—are erected out in the middle of nowhere, converting corn into clean energy. It's beautiful."

"I don't think I can."

"We will fly you out," he said.

"No, no. I don't fly."

Clark made some kind of crack, but I was looking at Julian, who had raised his eyebrows.

"Well, take a train. Rent a car. Do whatever you have to," he said. "Get on up to Omaha this week. It isn't all that far a drive, I bet. You're over there in Missouri, right?"

"Yes, but—"

"Well, hell, that's only a few hours away." He had me. I was going. "We'll give you the grand tour. Show you the whole shebang."

I agreed and told him I looked forward to meeting face-to-face.

"What was that all about?" Julian asked as I hung up.

I sighed. "A client in Omaha is pissed."

"Ah, who gives a shit?" Julian shrugged off what I did. His business thrived, year after year, without help from someone like me, someone in advertising. As any great friend would, he never let me hear the end of it.

"I give a shit," I told him. "If we lose this account, I'm fucked."

Julian rolled his eyes.

"So did you make it last night?" I took the opportunity to turn things around on him.

"Just barely." He shook his head. "For being knocked up, that fucking gal is quick on her feet. I figured by now she'd have given up."

"I bet."

Julian looked over his shoulder, distracted by my assistant. I realized he was here out of midday boredom, nothing more.

"Have you seen the legs on that secretary of yours?" He gave a kind of whistle and settled back into his chair, turning toward me.

"We're supposed to call them administrative assistants."

"Call her whatever you have to. I want those legs wrapped around me." He held out his hands as he would if he were spreading her open. "Those strong, throbbing thighs, that creamy center steaming for me." He actually licked his lips.

"Jesus Christ." I laughed, feeling strangely jealous at the thought of having to share her with him.

"What? I'm a man. It's only natural."

"Aren't you in enough trouble over things like that?"

"People are always getting in trouble for their religion." He spoke sincerely, not showing even a twinge of sarcasm or intended amusement.

"So women are your religion now?"

"They always have been." He was deadpan.

"And pussy is what? The Eucharist or something?" Drawing me into vulgarity had always been Julian's specialty.

"Exactly. You can't blame a Buddhist for meditating or a Muslim for fasting, can you?"

I shrugged.

"You know you can't. That's just the way the world works," he said. "Some men go to church every Sunday. Others walk on fire or speak in tongues. Some men are snake handlers. Me? I'm a skank handler."

We both burst out laughing.

I summoned Alicia, and she brought in a silver tray, arranged neatly with porcelain cups on saucers around a matching pot of coffee and cream dispenser. I watched Julian eyeing her as she came and went. He listened to her ask how we took it, staring at the curves of her arm, probably imagining life beneath that elegant pencil skirt and blouse, then he smiled up at her, a charming and genuine smile, before settling back into his chair with his cup and saucer.

I thanked her, and we both watched her go. Her legs were taught, slender but clearly defined despite the shadows of her charcoal tights. She walked expertly in her heels, elegantly and with short steps.

"Something, huh?" I said.

"Sure is." He leaned back and sipped at his coffee, filling the room with suckling sounds and the wisps of cooling exhales through pursed lips.

I smiled, knowing what I knew of Alicia, what Julian must have suspected because he grinned right back at me as he held the steaming coffee on his knee. As we exchanged looks, I knew we were thinking, as we so often did, the exact same thing. We often communicated through glimmers and faint, coy smiles instead of words. The office wasn't the place to go into details, but I was glad he knew. It was always a pleasure to stir even the slightest twinge of jealousy in him.

"Seriously, though, what was all that about?" he asked me. "With the phone call, I mean. I'm genuinely curious."

"This client in Omaha is being needy," I told him. "I'll probably head over there tomorrow morning."

"To Nebraska?"

"Yeah."

"Do you have to?" He sounded like a child who didn't want to be left alone.

"We might lose the account if I don't. The guy wants me there as soon as possible. I might even leave tonight."

"You're going to drive, aren't you?"

"Of course," I said, trying to imagine how far away Omaha could be.

"My God, you're a pussy." He laughed, something I had expected.

"Why?"

"You're still afraid of flying."

"I'm not afraid," I said.

"Bullshit." He leaned back and crossed his legs, resting his ankle on the other knee. "When was the last time you flew?"

"I don't really have to," I said. "Most of our clients are right here in the Midwest."

"And it never occurred to you that your little five-hour drives to Chicago would only take an hour if you flew?"

"I'd rather drive, that's all."

"Do you think Josey Wales was afraid of flying?"

"The cowboy?"

"The man!" He was growing passionate, leaning forward and emphasizing his points with his hands. "Do you think 007 says, 'Hey, can you wait a second until my Dramamine kicks in?' when he's in a fucking dogfight?"

"What does that have to do with anything?"

"I'm just saying it's emasculating," he said decisively and then settled back.

"Do you want to come, or what?" I asked.

"To Nebraska? Thanks, but no thanks." He looked back to the portrait of the young Victorian girl drinking Coca-Cola.

"We could make a weekend out of it," I said, which piqued his interest. "What are you going to do here while I'm gone?"

"I've got a lot going on around the office," he lied, and I could tell.

"I was thinking it would be nice to get out of the city," I said. "See a little bit of the open road."

"I guess I should try to lie low for a while," he told me as though we hadn't been lying low for six months. "Getting out of the city wouldn't be so bad," he added, and then slapped his knee. "Let's do it. I could use a vacation."

Having won this rare little victory, I smiled and pressed the button for Alicia.

"Maybe ol' Maria might ease up the search after a few days of coming up with nothing." Julian sat back, considering this for a moment. "How the hell do you think she found us last night anyway?"

"She probably has spies all over town," I said. "One of the guys in the kitchen might have been her cousin. Either way, I doubt a weekend out of town is going to make this whole problem go away."

"Couldn't hurt."

"You're going to have to face it eventually, Julian."

"What are you," he replied, "my mother?"

CHAPTER 10

November 15, 1997

Julian's great uncle Jack had collapsed on a Wednesday evening when he was seventy-six. He had been a strong man all his life, a brute, physically active beyond what can be expected for a man who drank that much, but in the end, it was his heart that failed him. His entire body had been swollen, large and tough with the calloused skin of a rhinoceros. Shaking his hand was like having yours crushed between two dusty bricks, and I always hated to do it.

Jack and his younger brother Michael had never officially retired from the family business and kept offices in Vandeventer that they rarely visited. The two were men and acted accordingly, genuinely enjoying the taste of whiskey and eating the biggest, bloodiest steaks they could find. They also built things with their bare hands: a treehouse for Julian high above his backyard and massive wooden decks on the backs of their houses and the houses of their adult children.

The hospital waiting room was filled with family—and me, of course, because Julian and I were together when he'd received the news—who all waited up until word came at two o'clock in the morning that Great Uncle Jack had passed on.

When the doctor delivered the news, Jack's grandchildren began to weep, and Julian's mother gathered her teenaged son into her arms. Like my own mother, she had never needed or wanted a man after her husband had died, although she never developed the habits of the perpetually single. Instead, she had retained her beauty, that long black hair and smooth skin. There was scarcely a hint of crow's feet when she smiled, and her body maintained the balletic slenderness of a woman half her age. Her husband had died sixteen years earlier, and each anniversary of his death so closely accompanied the birthday celebration of her son that it was a wonder she could ever manage. But manage she did, and despite never wanting or needing a man beyond her son, she still maintained an appearance so striking that men of all ages continued to fawn over her.

I had fantasized about her, admittedly, but in that moment, as I leaned onto the arm of the hospital waiting room chair, my chin cupped in my hand, the inevitable carnal imaginings that plague every teenaged boy were the furthest thing from my mind. Instead, I thought about how quickly a man's flaws were forgotten once he left this world. Sure, the man who lay dead a short walk down the hallway was their own flesh and blood, but he certainly fell far shy of perfection. Julian was beginning to cry then, and I thought of how it was as if everyone were overcome with Alzheimer's or amnesia when anyone dies.

They all stood there weeping, clearly forgetting the rampant drunkenness, the womanizing. It was as if all the negative things in his life were washed away, sins purged by death. Even the events of just a year before, those still fresh in everyone's minds, were forgiven. I couldn't understand how they had all forgotten—or at least ignored—that week he had disappeared, leaving the office one afternoon and not turning up at home.

The police were called, and a missing persons file was opened. The entire family was in pieces, fearing he had been killed or worse. That was until they found him in a suite at the Lodge of Four Seasons at Lake of the Ozarks. He had requested the housekeepers not attend to his room so that by the time he was discovered, every inch of available counter space, the top of every end and coffee table, was covered with empty bottles. Julian told me, nearly bragging, that they had found a dozen different kinds of whiskey and enough Budweiser to drown even the most dedicated drunks in the same time frame. He apparently had some MS Contin on him as well, 100 mg of morphine sulfate in each little white tablet.

The resort manager said that Jack would spend hours floating on a raft out on the lake, bobbing up and down in the water with his eyes closed, never venturing too far from the cooler of beer he kept on the marina dock. I imagined him taking the morphine and heading down to the lake, his bulbous body floating with the same indifference to his surroundings as a waterlogged piece of wood.

And despite all of that, Jack was still revered, not only by his family but by the whole of St. Louis as well. Even though some fifty-five years had passed since his heroics in Italy, he was still considered a first son of the city. By noon that Thursday, less than ten hours after his death, before the obituary had even been written, the city council of St. Louis held an impromptu meeting to confer honors on their fallen son. They composed a formal writ printed on parchment with swirling calligraphic type, the seal of St. Louis—an ornate steamship churning upstream surrounded with gild—at the top. The document decreed that an avenue be named in honor of Jack Lally, and the council and the mayor had signed it before it was framed behind glass and presented to Jack's surviving sons on the day of the funeral.

He had been good to his family, I guess, providing for them financially to make up for a lack of affection. He was cold and distant, coarse and harsh, and I guess that was where his embodiment of manliness truly lay. At all events, Julian loved him. He was a father figure to the young boy, the man Julian preferred to his own grandfather, a preference I suspect was reciprocated because Jack always seemed to dote on Julian more than his own grandchildren.

It's well known that fatherless sons collect father figures, even in the animal kingdom. When bull elephants approach adulthood, they grow increasingly violent and aggressive, just as human teenagers do, and they are overwhelmed by attacks of musth, which means madness in Hindi, to which they respond by leaving their mothers and going out into the wild. These bull elephants are walking testosterone, the mark of their musth cycle a green pus that runs down their right hind legs and smells like freshly cut grass. In the wild, this musth alerts elder male elephants, which then act as mentors, father figures, who guide the younger elephants and teach them how to use their strength to better benefit their tribe.

There is a void we fatherless sons need to fill, one that our mothers can't begin to satisfy. Mine was inadequately filled by two uncles, men with their own sons who didn't care much for me. My mother would encourage them to take me for the afternoon, to a ball game or the park for an awkward game of catch. In the moment, I always felt happy and whole. They would smile down at me and impart some nugget of information about baseball or manhood. Eventually, though, I would talk too much or they wouldn't have enough time for me. I would cry, and my mother would hug and console me as she plotted another potential role model to replace my absentee father. But with each role model, I grew less interested, becoming disillusioned with each of them as I unwrapped their imperfections.

Men aren't bull elephants. Our instincts aren't ingrained in us by nature because we are creatures regulated by example. And when that example is a flawed, selfish, and unfit father figure who is no more qualified than a stranger chosen at random, we fatherless sons find only flaws in them as, over time, their true character comes to the surface. What a seven-year-old takes as gospel, a ten-year-old starts to doubt, and a fourteen-year-old knows is bullshit. It is inevitable. Given enough time, these dynamics always end in disappointment.

Great Uncle Jack was certainly Julian's father figure, though whereas I had been all too quickly disillusioned, Julian held onto his deep love for his uncle even in death. None of the negative traits mattered. What was important to him was that this man had cared for him enough to occasionally pick him up and let him be his gopher while he did a project on his house. I was with Julian once when Jack had arrived randomly one Saturday to pick him up. I was invited, reluctantly, to come along and lend a helping hand. I think we were twelve at the time.

We backed out of the driveway in Jack's old '89 Chevrolet, a boxy white pickup that carried the honorable marks of use. Despite having money, Jack, unlike everyone else in his family, didn't spend it unless he had to.

"Why would I want a truck too nice to use?" he responded when I asked him something stupid about buying a new one.

As we sped, rattling and shaking, on our way to the hardware store, I kept on challenging and asking Great Uncle Jack questions. He was drinking beer from a can as he drove, and I could tell I was irritating him.

"Can I trust your little friend here, Julian?" he said finally.

Julian smiled and told him yes.

"Now, Brad, is it?" Uncle Jack opened another beer and put it between his knees as he drove on.

"Brett."

He didn't hear me or didn't care. "Some things aren't meant for women's ears," he went on. "Understand?"

I didn't, but I nodded.

"My boys and I have always lived by this kind of code. I shared it with your buddy Julian a few years ago. When we get to talking, us men all together working like this, nothing leaves the room. Okay, son?"

This was the first time I could recall having ever been called "son" by an older man. It didn't sound right. I looked to Julian, who was watching his uncle admiringly, hanging on every word.

"It's called man talk," Uncle Jack continued. "And no woman needs to hear about it."

That afternoon, as we picked up splinters of wood and bent nails and swept sawdust off the floor of his garage, I heard words no twelve-year-old should. The man cursed like an old salt, and I realized that "man talk" was his way of not getting himself into trouble with Julian's mother. To this day, Julian claims he held countless meaningful man talks with his great uncle. I attribute it to that blindness that accompanies undying adoration. There was nothing special about that man. Hell, there probably is nothing special about any man, and yet fatherless boys worship them, and, on that special instance when they live up to even half of the expectations we have of fathers, we're too blind to become disillusioned, continuing to revere them as the men we try to resemble despite all their flaws.

In any event, it was decided that Julian be among the pallbearers at Great Uncle Jack's funeral, carrying the black casket by the pearl handles alongside the man's two sons and three of his nephews from his wife's side of the family. The November day was cold and overcast in the morning, and by the time the services began, the north wind had carried in an icy drizzle that coated the handrails leading up the church steps of the Cathedral Basilica of St. Louis and numbed my fingers.

The funeral opened with a mass and benedictions, the details of which I cannot recall since the emerald dome of the cathedral and its high arches covered with golden mosaics held my interest for the ass-numbing two hours of elongated amens.

Once the priest had finished up the absolution, the procession to the grave started, led by Julian and the five others deemed worthy enough to carry the great Jack Lally to his final repose. When they passed our pew, all eyes followed the casket down the aisle and beneath the extravagant archways supporting the choir loft and silver pipe organ, some forty feet above the heads of the congregation. I, however, was looking at my friend, intently studying his face, a face visibly burdened by the heavy load of his dead great uncle. He wore a black suit and tie as comfortably as a boy could with that much weight in his arms.

My mother and I snaked out the front of the church along with the hundreds of men and women in black, lagging behind the coffin. I could see them from the top of the stairs, umbrellas crowding around, canopying out the wintry rain. The men and Julian slid the casket into the hearse.

After we found our car, my mother and I followed the long procession north, the police escort leading the hearse and more than two hundred mourners. I still remember how our windshield wipers squeaked, and the heater did the best it could to keep the cold from opaquing the emergency flashers of the car directly in front of us. My mother tried to make small talk by explaining the history of the cemetery we were headed to.

"Kate Chopin and Tennessee Williams are buried up here in Calvary," she said, noticing possibly that my hands were cupped together between my thighs. This was, as best I can recall, my first funeral, and my mother could see the impact this grand macabre spectacle was having on me. So she did what she did best and lightened the mood by taking my mind off what lay ahead.

Calvary Cemetery was lined with ornate and massive mausoleums, worn stonework marking the graves of St. Louis' best, brightest, and wealthiest. We followed the procession in and parked, sinking in the sopping grass and mud as we crowded to the cemetery plot along with everyone else. The rain was coming down steadily now, drumming loudly against the top of the tent covering the open grave. The mob of onlookers huddled around, angling between shoulders for a view of the hearse that had pulled up alongside the tent. The pallbearers, Julian among them, stood shoulder to shoulder and pulled the coffin from the hearse, then placed it on the lowering device and stepped back. The Lally family sat in chairs neatly rowed, shielded from the rain by the tent above. I stood on my tiptoes, peering over a hunched man's shoulder, curious to see what was happening.

"I am the Resurrection and the Life," the priest said as Great Uncle Jack disappeared into the ground. The priest sprinkled the grave with water, blessing the hole as he circled it and repeated: "I am the Resurrection and the Life."

I noticed Julian then, and he was shaking. He was choking back tears, his hand held to his face in an attempt to mask the shame of his outpouring of emotions. The men on either side of him, Jack's own sons who were molded in Jack's great image of the quintessential man, stood with their shoulders square, their faces stoic and stern, as they watched their father fall into the afterlife.

The priest went on, calling on us to recite the Lord's Prayer. Julian did everything he could to choke back the sadness at the loss of this man, this father figure. I knew as I watched him sniffle, his chin shaking, eyes affixed to the opened ground before him where the casket had been lowered, that he was ashamed of his tears. And yet his sobs grew louder, intermingling and becoming almost indiscernible from the feminine blubbering and whimpering of Jack's young nieces and granddaughters, and I realized then that he was the only pallbearer, the only man, to cry.

"May his soul," the priest went on, "and the souls of all the faithful departed, through the mercy of God, rest in peace."

Then there was silence, save for the rain and Julian's pathetic, muffled sobs.

CHAPTER 11

...MICE, MEN, AND THE REST OF US

On Thursday, I worked until noon before renting a car for the long haul to Omaha. I had insisted on a convertible and imagined this as some sort of adventure, an attempt to capture a glimpse of masculine Middle America. As I prepared for the trip, I felt myself being swept up by it all, inevitably thinking of Hunter S. Thompson and his trip across the desert to that most decadent and wholly American oasis. However, I figured it best to forgo the cache of drugs and the gun and simply packed a few suits and casual summer wear.

As I pulled onto Julian's street in exclusive Frontenac, I recalled a saying attributed to Samuel Johnson: "He who makes a beast of himself gets rid of the pain of being a man." I looked forward to that, though I hoped we could keep a bit of our composure. I had no desire to end up immortalized as some Ralph Steadman monster the way Thompson was, all mouths and bloodshot eyes spewing splotches of ink-red madness across the page.

The wide driveway in front of Julian's townhouse was steep and so fresh and white that it looked like bleached shale, and as I sat waiting—of course he made me wait—with the top down, I began to bake in the summer sun and felt myself sticking to the leather seat. It had been only seconds, but I was eager to get on the road, so I laid on the horn of the BMW 335i convertible. I had been hoping for red (like the Thompson book), but the BMW was charcoal with burnt-tan seats that smelled of polished leather. It was shaped like a cruise missile and hummed sweetly each time I massaged the gas pedal with my foot.

"You know this thing barely has a trunk, right?" I said as Julian walked toward the car, a suitcase the size of a small refrigerator in tow behind him. He had another overstuffed bag hanging from his shoulder that was so visibly overstuffed that I expected the seams to burst.

Julian laughed as he pushed a pair of sunglasses up the bridge of his nose. He wore a white cotton polo, opened wide at the collar, the skin over his sunken clavicles tanned like milk chocolate. I hit the button, and the trunk made a sound like suction releasing followed by a ping as it popped open. I cranked up the air conditioning, feeling the blast of cool air wash over my face and escape out the openness of the convertible. Julian rummaged and banged around in the trunk, struggling to force his bulky suitcase inside.

"That took some doing," Julian said as he fell into the seat next to me with the squeak of his weight on the leather.

He closed his door, and we were off, weaving north through the suburbs of St. Louis. At I-70, I merged in with the afternoon traffic like a tributary feeding into a great river heading west.

"So what's the plan?" Julian was hunched forward in his seat, fiddling with the knobs and buttons of the rental car, amused and entertained by the simple pleasure of something new and different.

"I don't have to meet with our client in Omaha until noon tomorrow," I explained. "I've got it all worked out so I only have to spend Friday with these people. I figure we'll make it to Kansas City sometime around seven tonight, then check into the hotel and hit the town."

"I see." He sounded bored. "When will we be coming back?"

"That's up to you," I said.

"Are you wanting to check out Omaha?"

"I guess."

I hadn't really considered it. The road was captivating me. I was enjoying the wind on my face and the way my hair whipped about. We sat in silence for some time, and I watched as the city running alongside the highway grew smaller, the buildings gradually sifting apart and giving way to the cookie-cutter houses and chain eateries of the deep suburbs, which were then themselves gradually split, wider and wider, by the growing rural expanse of the middle of this great country. By Wentzville, the interstate opened up, and at Wright City, we saw the first livestock of the trip. At Warrenton, there was an outlet mall, the crowning pinnacle of the American dream: whatever you desire made cheap, sold even cheaper in bulk, the landmark of convenience.

We sped through the cascading Missouri countryside, and I looked for deer in the smearing green blur of fields as we tore across the state. I was mesmerized by the flow of yellow and white lines on the pavement and the billboards rising up out of the natural beauty of the lush, open spaces.

"I'd like to do something new," Julian said as we passed Danville.

"We're heading someplace we've never been," I said, checking my mirrors and changing lanes to pass a soot-covered semi. "Isn't that new enough for you?"

Julian shrugged.

"I hear what you're saying, though. That thing with that asshole Cubs fan the other night got me thinking. Day in, day out we do the same things. We watch baseball, and we make money. We eat well and dress well, then we drink and meet women."

"Yeah, our lives do sound pretty great when you put it like that." Julian smiled, leaning his head back to let the hair dance around his face on the wind, the rays of light gleaming off the tint of his sunglasses.

"I just think we're missing something," I told him.

"What more could there be?"

"That's what I'm trying to tell you."

He could tell I was annoyed and kept poking the buttons, needling me in the way men and best friends do. Breaking each other's balls as often as possible.

"There are things we have never tried —"

"Are you coming onto me?" He was already laughing before I could even tell him to piss off.

"We talk so much about how men like Lee Van Cleef lived their lives," I went on as I mounted my little soapbox. It felt surprisingly sincere. "We always talk about what it means to be a man, asking what John Wayne or Charles Bronson might do. We talk about these men and about how we're men, but we don't do anything—at least none of the things that real men do."

"What do you mean?"

"Like fishing," I said. "I've never been fishing. I think real men go out with their pole, haul in a huge fish, and then gut it right there on the side of the bank."

"That sounds pretty gross."

"I'm sure it is. But it's what men do." I was getting excited about the possibilities.

"So you want to go fishing?"

"Sure. Why the hell not?"

Julian sat silent for a moment. I gripped the steering wheel and felt the sweat of my palms on the taut leather, the highway beneath us.

"I've never been fishing." He tilted his head back and considered it. "I'm not sure I want to go fishing."

"Forget the fucking fishing," I groaned. "I just want to do something, anything, that lives up to the things we talk about."

"So what do you suggest?" Julian said

"I don't know," I said as I bit the inside of my cheek. "But it ought to be something, well, manly. Something bold and strong and even courageous."

Even as I spoke, I knew how abstract these goals were and how little is accomplished when friends talk of lofty ideas and dreams. Best laid plans, you know. And yet, in that moment, I felt as if something big were about to happen. It seemed, for a change, we were on the right track, that what lay before was going to transform us for the better. All we had to do was go out in search of what had been missing and maybe prove something to ourselves.

Just past Ridge Prairie, we stopped at a gas station to fill up. The restroom smelled like urine masked with ammonia, and my feet made little sticking sounds as if I were walking with drying gum on the bottom of my shoes. I stood far back from the porcelain urinal and arced it in because the entire thing was stained yellow and the rim was covered with squiggly tendrils of dark pubic hair. There were so many of them, so many stray hairs, that I wondered what sad, sorry man out there was fighting crotch baldness. It was bad enough to lose the hair on your head, to look ridiculous out in public. (And don't let anyone fool you. Bald men aren't appealing. Their heads look like shiny topographical maps in all the varying shapes a potato is known to have.) But to lose the hairs of your plot? Becoming like a nine-year-old boy again might be too much to take. The cruelties of a man's world are endless.

I met Julian by the counter of the gas station, where he was paying for a plastic sack of food and drinks. At the car, I handed him the keys to the BMW because he wanted to drive, and we set off again, following the setting sun west as it fell imperceptibly toward the horizon.

Julian held the wheel with one hand as he dug through his bag, the ruffling sound of plastic audible even over the winds of the interstate.

"You want half of my chicken salad sandwich?" Julian asked as he pulled out a wedge, some sort of white mess, wrapped in clear plastic.

"God, no," I said. "Especially not from a gas station."

"Looks benign enough to me." He examined the sandwich from all angles.

"I have gone my entire life without eating chicken that has been puréed and whipped to the point where it can be called salad. And I think I'd like to keep it that way."

"Suit yourself." Julian shrugged, then pushed in a bite of sandwich larger than his mouth and choked it down.

I leaned back and nestled into the headrest, then watched the world go by.

"Oh, God," Julian exclaimed.

"That good?"

"No." He reached for his bottle of water. "It's awful."

I laughed at him.

"Get it away from me." He held out the sandwich box. "Quarantine that immediately."

I took the second half of the sandwich and mashed it in with all the rest of the garbage in the door compartment. Julian made faces, working his tongue around in his mouth in a desperate search for any sandwich particles that remained stuck in his teeth. He groaned and laughed.

"The taste is sticking to my sinuses. I can't get it out."

"The saddest part of that whole sandwich is that chickens had to die," I said. "A tragedy that actual chickens were harmed in the making of such a heinous, mayonnaise-riddled glob."

"Do I regret the sandwich?" he asked himself, still trying to suck the taste from his gums. "Of course I do. Would I have eaten it knowing what I know now? Hell no! But tomorrow will come, then the next day. Time will go on. And I tell you something, my friend, the day will come again when I gamble on chicken salad," he continued, fueled by my laughter. "One day, I will be walking through a gas station and see a chicken salad sandwich, and I will completely forget what has transpired here today until I take that first, rotten bite."

I was in stitches.

"You can be assured —" he hawked and spat out the open window "— that I will someday be walking through a Phillips 66, and I'll look down and see a sandwich just like that one, handmade that very day by a teenaged kid with a plastic name tag and a beard of acne or a white-trash minx with skid marks, and I will pick it up, saying to myself, 'Yum! Chicken salad sandwich—that sounds delicious!'"

"You're like an Alzheimer's patient," I said through tears.

We arrived in Kansas City at sunset, lurching into town with traffic. I took off my sunglasses and watched the sun fall behind the hodgepodged skyline of awkwardly mismatched and unsightly buildings. There was nothing redeeming about any of it: a turd-brown high-rise with a massive corporate logo on the side next to squat, colorless buildings, behind which rose four aluminum-colored spires tied together by giant crisscrossing cables. I thought it might be a suspension bridge, but Julian explained that it was the convention center. It looked so out of place in a city whose skyline didn't look like a city at all but rather a vomitous mix of all the skylines of modern America. I was horrified.

As Julian led us away from I-70 and onto Emanuel Cleaver II Boulevard, I turned up the radio and listened to the lilting cadence of George Harrison singing about his sweet lord. I leaned my head back to stare skyward and take in the air of Kansas City.

"Do you smell that?" I said as I snapped my head upright. We were in the thick of dilapidated housing projects, and the road was jarring and narrow. To our left was a sad river of gray water that was choked with garbage and brush.

"Yeah," Julian said, crinkling his face. "What is that?"

"It smells like farts."

"And barbecue," Julian said as we drove past the fifteen-foot-tall black statue in front of Gates Bar-B-Q that was cast to look like he was eternally strutting forward with his cane and top hat.

"This city smells like farts and barbecue," I said.

A wiser man might have recognized this as indicative of things to come. Julian and I weren't wise men. Instead, we simply laughed and covered our noses with our shirts and agreed to put the top of the BMW back up the first chance we got.

CHAPTER 12

A BULL NAMED KIKI LA VELVA

We pulled into the circle drive of the Raphael, a nine-story upscale hotel built of rust-colored brick and white stone, and rounded a bed of pink and white tulips before parking beneath a velvety red awning framed by flowering trees. Julian tossed the valet our keys, then motioned the bellhop over to take our bags. Once inside the lobby, we checked in quickly then Julian turned to me.

"I'll be right back," he said as I handed him a room key.

"Where are you going?" I demanded, but he just gave me a slight wave and disappeared around the corner, so I shrugged and followed the bellhop up to our room.

Typically, my nights traveling around the Midwest were spent in Holiday Inns, but Julian had refused to, as he called it, slum. He would rather pay for a room out of his pocket than to bed up for the night in the same place as a traveling soccer team or a family on vacation. As for me, I wasn't going to turn down a free four-star hotel room.

Our fifth-floor room featured plush, queen-sized beds beneath arching windows that overlooked the Country Club Plaza, and I looked down on the headlights that flowed through the streets. There was also a wide section of Brush Creek walled beautifully with ornate stones and manicured grass. It was serene, the water a perfect mirror that reflected the lights of the Plaza and the city, and I wondered how this could possibly be connected to the same cesspool we had seen and smelled when we first arrived.

The door clicked open a few minutes later, and Julian entered and kicked his luggage with the side of his foot as he passed it, pushing it next to a wall-length mirror. He plopped onto his bed and felt the mattress with his fingertips, then rolled onto his back and spread out, his palms open as if he were on a crucifix of goose down.

"What are we going to do tonight?" I took a seat in the corner chair and put my feet up.

"I thought you'd never ask," Julian said, still staring skyward. I watched him smile, then try to do a kip-up by placing his hands flat by his ears, arching his back, and kicking up hard. His right hand slipped, and he landed flat on his back where he had started. Instead of giving it another go, he casually rolled onto his side to face me. "I got you a present," he said, his elbow on the bed, and his cheek resting in his hand.

I said something stupid like, "Huh."

Julian rolled off his bed and pulled two long tickets from his pocket, handing them to me. Above the price and section number, I saw the logo, a red silhouette of a cowboy riding atop a bucking bronco. In the foreground, arching above the rider and his horse, was block lettering: IGRA.

"Is this for a rodeo?"

"Yeah," Julian said, outwardly satisfied with himself. "I got to thinking about what you said earlier in the car. You know, about doing manly stuff. So I talked to one of the gals downstairs. She told me that the rodeo was in town."

"And she had tickets right there?"

"Yeah." He fell back onto his bed again, swimming on the comforter. "Apparently the Kemper Arena drops off tickets for every event. Last time I stayed here they had concert tickets. Incidentally, the girl down there is gorgeous. A fiery little minx."

"Of course she is," I said in an attempt to sidestep the same old conversation. "Are you sure you want to go to a rodeo?"

"Sure," he said. "Why not?"

"I don't know. It just seems so... rural. So country. I'm not sure we're really country."

"You wanted to do something manly. This thing is going to have some of the toughest guys in the world riding bulls. Fucking bulls! Have you ever seen one in real life? We might see somebody get gored tonight."

The prospect sounded entertaining in a savage sort of way. I felt a flush of excitement at the thought of such violence and decided that this exhilaration was what men were supposed to feel and even seek out.

The two of us took turns showering, then argued about what we were supposed to wear. Neither of us had a cowboy hat or boots, though we agreed that was probably for the best. Julian suggested we go buy something, but there was no time. So we dressed casually, I in a linen shirt with the sleeves cuffed, Julian in a polo, and we both wore shorts.

Drinking was a given, so we decided it best to hail a cab. There were none waiting at the entrance of the Raphael, however, so Julian proclaimed that I really had to see the Plaza, and we took off in that direction. The air smelled fresh and sweet in this part of town, and the Country Club Plaza, which was really an outdoor mall finished like a baroque city of ornate towers and stucco, was alive with people—families herding children, couples on their way to dinner reservations, suburban wives and daughters toting armfuls of shopping bags. Everyone was beautiful and well-dressed and white.

As we walked, Julian explained that the shopping center was built with European influences, and he pointed to the Giralda Tower, with its florid spires rising above the district. The area had been modeled after Seville, and the tower was an almost exact replica of the cathedral there. The sidewalks were clean, and there were fountains everywhere.

At the corner of JC Nichols Parkway and the four lanes of 47th Street, we finally stopped in front of P.F. Chang's to hail a cab. The food smelled fantastic, but I was eager to get a drink. As Julian waved at the passing cabs, I looked at the sunbaked stucco walls of the building that housed the Chinese bistro. Between the rumbles and honks of passing traffic, I could hear the dousing fountains, the splashing water filling the air with showering licks.

"Brett," Julian hollered from the curb. "Let's go."

Merging into traffic, then turning up Main Street toward downtown Kansas City, we sped past another fountain that sat on a great lawn and was surrounded by people. There were children who scrambled about as they chased one another, couples who walked hand in hand, a vagabond with a shopping cart, and a few people who paused to toss coins in and make a wish. I tried to take in the whirlwind of life in that park as we sped past, but it was all gone too quickly, the beautiful scene fading and leaving Julian and me and the taxi driver to ride in silence through the fluorescent and neon mosaic heart of the bright city.

"So what are we going to do about the whole one-bedroom thing?" Julian asked later as we merged onto Southwest Trafficway.

"You're expecting us to pick up women at a rodeo?"

Julian shrugged, and I noticed the taxi driver eavesdropping and thought about telling him to mind his own business. I was feeling tough, manly, aggressive, and I wanted to exert my authority like the dominant lion in a pride. But instead, I just lowered my voice a bit.

"I'm not sure these are going to be our kind of girls," I said, picturing elephantine plaid shirts that struggled and stretched to cover the sort of women who might enjoy the smell of manure, the sight of livestock, the sound of country music.

"Let's not rule anything out," Julian said with a smile. "I've never been one to refuse the grateful type."

"We could have gotten two rooms, you know?"

"You the one paying?"

"You're a strange man," I said and paused for a moment. "I figure one of us will just let the other have the room if it comes to that."

"And if things get started while the other is in the room?"

"Well, then it should work just like that time at the lake," I told him, though I hoped we weren't the same men we had been four years earlier.

"Ah," he said with lilting nostalgia. "No joining in until you're waved in?"

"Christ," I said, conscious that the cabbie was listening and drawing his own conclusions. "Fine."

As the taxi crested a hill, we saw the Kemper Arena rise before us, a lonely blip centered in a district that once held the stockyards, the liveliest and fastest-moving area in the Midwest. The flatlands were empty now, nothing but orphan rail lines and the bulky white arena that looked like the rest of Kansas City: a bumbling and gawky building obviously altered to look updated but instead stuck somewhere in 1974. Green and white lights, aimed upward like spotlights for a bad movie premiere, illuminated the white cross sections of massive poles built to hold up the roof and reflected off five stories of sloped glass. At night, it was almost beautiful in its awkwardness.

The sidewalks were surprisingly empty given the nature of the event. I had expected a sea of wide-brimmed cowboy hats teetering upon bodies sheathed in burly plaid tucked into Levi's beneath, all meandering through the turnstiles. But there was no line, no fanfare. Instead, it was only the two of us. I figured everyone else must already be inside.

We made our way through opened glass doors and did our dance with the ticket takers at the turnstiles. Then we rounded the outer concourse under the banners for the Kansas City Scouts, the Blades, and the Knights, teams I had never heard of and apparently didn't exist anymore. One could tell that this old barn had once been home to some great events. It was a grandiose arena that could hold almost twenty thousand people but probably never would again. I tried to imagine the old days when there were fans, when the events and contests here drew sellout crowds. I could hear a crackling PA and the muffled hooting and hollering that constituted the rodeo's pathetic excuse for cheering and discovered that, strange as it might seem, I felt sorry for the building because it was washed up, behind the times, and unwanted.

Julian bought us a couple of beers from an old man dotted with moles. Then we walked through the tunnel and out into the open air of the arena bowl. The stadium seating, though only sparsely attended, held thousands of wide-backed men leaning forward in their chairs, mesmerized by the livestock and cowboys dancing around on the clumps of dirt in the oval ring.

Our row, with the exception of a group of men we had to bump past to find our seats, was nearly empty. I expected eyes to be on us and judging whispers to follow. We were outsiders, after all, and looked as such. But I was wrong. I couldn't have been more wrong. Our arrival, our presence at the rodeo, dressed out of place in our preppy shorts and dress shirts, was instead met with welcoming nods and polite smiles. In that moment, I found it refreshing that, in this day and age, people could be so accepting, welcoming even. Rather than being eyed and judged, Julian and I were toasted. The crowd of men in the rows around us, sporting their ten-gallon hats and Wranglers, held up their Budweisers in smiling approval. I had worried we would be heckled or worse, I guess. But that wasn't the case, and I was then reminded that, in their joviality at our joining in their reindeer games, these people, these rodeo-goers, were the most westerly culture of this West, said to be some of the most genial Americans out there. At the time, I was grateful.

I don't know much about rodeos—other than what I learned that night—but I think Julian and I missed the singing of the national anthem or whatever it is they do to kick things off. By the time we were settled in and sipping beer, the rodeo was well underway. I expected only bull riding, but in a rodeo, there was always a great deal more.

The first event was something called team roping, in which two riders, a header and a heeler, come out of their respective gates on horseback to chase a swiftly running steer. As the first set of cowboys bolted out of the gate, hoofing up russet dirt behind them, they sought the steer, the header aiming to rope the animal's horns, the heeler his back legs. And they were good, so good that each attempt was over in a flash and you were consistently left wanting more.

"Did you see that?" Julian elbowed me when the header of one team rode too fast as he roped the steer. He took it in tow so quickly that he nearly yanked the beast's head off as the tightened rope pulled its face into the earthen floor of the ring.

The team roping event was followed by something that the announcer called steer wrestling. This, I can honestly say, was one of the manliest, toughest things I had ever seen anyone do. I'm not sure if steer wrestling is something cowboys have to do often on a ranch or if it is merely an event done for entertainment. I'm willing to bet that the whole thing was invented by some bored wranglers who had been looking to fill the long, empty hours out on the open range and ultimately prove their cojones.

Regardless, the steer wrestler, or bulldogger, starts out on horseback behind the barrier, same as the team roping riders. The steer is released from the gate and given a head start. Then, with a bell, the wrestler chases it down, pulling alongside the steer and leaping from his horse onto the bovine before grasping it by the horns and digging his boot heels into the dirt to slow it down. Once the bulldogger has stopped the steer, he twists the horns to flip all hundreds and hundreds of pounds of prime beef onto its side. As I said, it was brutish and manly in a way I had never seen before.

I watched on in astonishment as the competitors, broad-shouldered men weighing two hundred plus pounds, vaulted off their horses then wrenched the thousand-pound steers onto their sides by the horns. It was a ridiculous feat of strength and force, these men violently twisting and pinning down running cattle, animals that outweighed them at least five to one. Julian and I could only watch, slowly sipping on our beers as we admired talents we couldn't hope to replicate. Even from thirty rows up, the dives of these cowboys looked incredibly gutsy, their manhandling of the walking beef stalwart.

"Need another one?" Julian asked, tipping back his empty cup and speaking into it as if it were a megaphone.

I said sure and continued to sit as he left for the concession stand. I was enraptured by these men among men who, night after night, proved their virility, their strength. The steer wrestling ended, and the barrelmen came out, clowns to fill the downtime, rolling out fiberglass drums, barrels twice the size of a man. They were the cheerleaders or halftime show. The barrelmen were slapstick, ridiculous clowns dancing and prancing in their parachute pants and face paint.

It was during the clowning session that I was approached. I was in my row, nearly empty save for the group of men down from us, and I looked to the man shuffling toward me with little bird steps.

"Are you enjoying the show?" he asked.

It was the first time I had heard a rodeo being referred to as a show. Now that he was closer, I could see that he was older, possibly in his fifties, with badly dyed hair the color of cinnamon. He was short, withered like crusted leather, but smiling, his crow's feet streaming from the corners of his eyes like tears.

I nodded to him and politely smiled.

"You don't seem like much of a cowboy." He seemed no cowboy himself but rather a bad forgery dressed in a western shirt with ivory-colored buttons.

My legs were crossed on the seat ahead of me. I didn't know what he wanted and figured he was talking to me because I appeared so out of place. Unable to discern then if he was about to wish me welcome or tell me to hit the bricks, I thought briefly of the Cubs fan and what Julian had said about fighting him. This man was thin, diminutive, scarcely a man by any means, and I felt a bit more confident should things turn that way.

"My name's Steven," he said. He reached his hand down, and I took it, shaking it vigorously and firmly, a gesture that wasn't returned. Steven's hand was so strangely soft, his palms tender and sweaty, and he held onto me gingerly.

"Nice to meet you," I said. "You're right. I'm no cowboy."

His voice was nasally and squeaked, and he said, "I'm in livestock insurance. When your horse quits breathin', call Steven."

"Thanks," I said, confusion mounting. "But I don't own any livestock."

He gave a sassy, tender laugh that didn't seem to belong to a man at all, then brushed my cheek with the back of his fingertips.

I grabbed his hand and threw it away from my face. "What the hell are you doing?"

"You really aren't a cowboy." Steven giggled.

"I think maybe you're confused about me," I said, feeling a bit squirmy and uncomfortable.

Steven shrugged and then did a flounced about-face before skipping down the stairs to his group of friends, who at once began chiding and flamboyantly mocking his rejection at my hands.

Maybe I should have been flattered, but that man, Steven, was souring everything Julian and I were trying to accomplish. Why were he and his friends, all of them gay men, so welcome at this manly affair?

I tried to settle back into the rodeo and forget anything had ever happened. Another event had begun, and men were strapping themselves onto the back of bulls and holding on for as long as they could out of the gate. Once the riders were thrown off, the barrelmen would distract the longhorns with their antics. The bull riding, the event we had come for, should have been the apex of our foray into the manly world of rodeos. And yet my run-in with Steven and his friends had left me feeling so sick, so betrayed by what I thought we were after that it had turned everything on its head. I viewed it all differently now.

Though the bulls in the riding event, or the steers in the other events, likely had no idea what humiliation was, they spent what little lives they had being humiliated. I'm not an activist or anything, but in that moment, all I could see was the cruelty in what they did to these magnificent animals solely for our entertainment. I mean, these beasts that exemplified the male, the masculine, were either ridden for kicks or castrated and then made a mockery of by being roped or wrestled to the ground. As a man— well, a man who is not of the cowboy ilk—you almost have to root for the bull or steer when they get loose.

"So, I definitely just saw two guys making out in the bathroom," Julian said as he handed me a fresh beer and fell into his folding arena seat.

I took the beer and drank. It tasted like Coors, smooth like cold water but with the skunky pungency of a foot. The taps were old, the kegs unused and settling into an expiring stink. I bumped Julian with my elbow and pointed a few rows down to two men who were tonguing, groping each other with vigor and passion. Red plaid bled into red plaid, hats tipped, the flaxen weavings like wicker bending and bumping together as the two men pressed against each other.

"I'm pretty sure we've made a mistake," I said.

Julian looked around, nodding as he took a long drink of his beer. In that moment, I noticed something that I hadn't picked up on before. Upon closer inspection, these cowgirls, dressed in Daisy Dukes and whatnot, weren't cowgirls at all. When we first arrived, I had thought they were thick, but it was a thickness I'd attributed to country fried steak. I realized then that there was a girth to their form, masculine shoulders and the jaws of linemen that drew up to rough, brutish faces framed by tussled wigs and rouged a deep self-conscious red.

"Our next rider," the PA whined and sputtered, "is out of San Angelo, Texas, and is riding Kiki La Velva."

Even the bulls had names out of a John Waters movie.

"You bought tickets to a gay rodeo," I said, and slugged Julian in the arm.

He rubbed his bicep through his sleeve without taking his eyes off the show around us.

"That girl at the hotel must have thought you were gay," I said, now laughing.

"Bullshit," he fired back, then paused. "I don't look queer, do I?"

I didn't think so, but I had only met a few of them in my lifetime. Most looked a lot like us: well dressed and put together, stylish you might say. Up until that point, I had never considered the fact that gay men could be cowboys too. And yet there we were, the only two straight men in a sea of homosexuals.

We watched a brute, built like a linebacker, as he was bucked off the back of a two-ton bull. The man, the gay man, was thrown off in a way that would have torn my arm right out of my shoulder, but he relished in it. His hat popped off his head, the dusty chaps kicking up with the dirt around his snakeskin boots as he scrambled away from the enraged bull. Three clowns danced around after it, waving their arms and stealing the bovine's attention. The rider sprinted to the iron fencing, then scrambled up to the top where he flipped over to safety. The crowd cheered on their feet as he raised his hand to wave and soak in their applause.

"I could never hope to be this tough," I admitted.

Julian nodded, staring straight forward at the show, the violent battle. I thought of the Roman Colosseum, the fights between beasts and men. They used to pit tigers and bears against armed slaves, cheering as they watched people get mauled and torn to bits of confetti.

"So we're the two biggest pussies at a gay rodeo?"

"I'm not sure sexual preference has all that much to do with it," I said.

"Yeah, but still. This may be one of the most emasculating moments of my young life," Julian said, taking in the amount of male handholding and snuggling going on in the seats around us. "I kind of always figured I was, you know, stronger than," he looked over both shoulders, "well, you know."

"I think most of these guys are tougher than your average football player, regardless of being gay. I know what you mean though."

"You don't think all of those gunmen and cowboys we used to idolize were closet queers, do you?"

"If they were," I said, "then I think we have been going about all of this ass-backwards."

"Ass-backwards," Julian repeated with a snicker, and took another long gulp of beer.

CHAPTER 13

WHEN THE WORLD RUNS ON CORN

I awoke early in our room at the Raphael the morning following the rodeo. Julian was still snoring, his head cocked back on his pillow, mouth open. Our room was an icebox, the air conditioning set as high as possible, so I snuggled up in the sheets, curling my knees to my chest as I stared at the menacing red eyes of the clock radio. It wasn't yet eight o'clock, and we had time before the trip to Omaha. I felt a dull ache in my throat, the starchy thirst of another hangover.

After the rodeo, we had taken to the town, "drinking the gay off us," as Julian called it. Julian knew Kansas City better than me and directed the cab driver to the Power & Light District, where we were dropped off at the base of the Sprint Center, a monstrosity of mirrored glass through which the uncomely reflection of the city lights glowed like the lightning bugs my mother and I used to catch and bottle in mason jars in Forest Park when I was a boy.

We wandered into the crowded atrium, walking side by side through a courtyard of beautiful stone, open to the night air though covered by an arched awning of steel and mesh and blue opaque glass with white lights hanging from the girders that dimly sketched the features of all of those faces that drank and flirted and danced and talked with one another.

The Power & Light District was a newly developed center of town built for the young, the scandalous, and the wealthy. It was a pedestrian mall the size of a small European village, the towering walls of which were composed of three levels of bars and restaurants. You could hop from bar to bar without hailing a cab or even leaving your last drink behind, and there were such girls, such wild girls, who were all polished and beautiful in the right light.

Julian and I spent an hour or so at Howl at the Moon, a piano bar where the performers sat at dueling grand pianos and played covers that ranged from Frank Sinatra to the timeless classic "Baby Got Back." After a few drinks, Julian suggested we leave because it was too loud to talk to anyone, save for each other when we laughed and shouted.

We decided to move to Lucky Strike, a swanky lounge and bowling alley in one that combined the elegance of a martini and the trashiness of wearing community shoes. A handful of college girls were in the lane next to us, and Julian went to work on them immediately. He may have come on too strong when he asked two of them to come back with us, but I think he was desperate to prove his heterosexuality after the rodeo fiasco. I just wanted to get drunk, and did. The night got blurry, but I remember Julian tongued one of the college girls and took down her phone number, and we ended the night alone—and gonorrhea-free—in the blasting air conditioning of our hotel room.

As the hangover settled in, I rolled out of bed, shivering, popped a handful of Aleve, and took a hot shower. After a shave, I tried to wake Julian, who responded by groaning and then rolling over to mash his face into the pillow.

"Let's go," I said, throwing open the curtains to let the morning light flood in. "Come on. I have to be there by noon."

"What am I supposed to do while you're off at your big meeting?" Julian asked, his voice muffled by the bedding.

"You're just going to stay here?" I demanded as I dug into my garment bag and picked a salmon-colored dress shirt with alternating thin blue stripes.

"What is there to do in Omaha, anyway?"

"No idea," I said, pinning the French cuffs of my shirt with cufflinks. "But I don't want to go alone."

"I think I'm going to relax here by the pool," Julian said before rolling over and hocking to clear the snot in his throat.

This annoyed me, but it was typical of Julian in a way. Having finished dressing, I left without another word, storming out of the hotel and taking off north out of downtown Kansas City on I-29. I kept the top up to ride in the crisp breeze of the AC and rolled along the Missouri hills, splitting the gaps of arched bluffs and blooming foliage.

I settled into the ride around St. Joseph, strumming my air guitar to Bachman-Turner Overdrive and belting out the lyrics to every Bruce Springsteen song I could find on the radio. Then I sang "na, na, na, na-na-na-na, na-na-na-na hey Jude" along with my favorite Beatle, Paul. A coworker had once given me their biography. He was a certifiable Beatlemaniac, which inevitably meant that he tried to spread the word of the Fab Four like some religious zealot spreads the word of Christ. Don't get me wrong, the Beatles are great, but I was never a maniac about much. I just couldn't get into the book, something I regretted as I drove north, wondering for a moment who Jude was. The real Jude, I mean. It must have been a woman, I decided, some lover who'd had her heart broken by Paul or one of the other Beatles.

I called Clark as I drove, and he walked me through directions to the restaurant. I followed the interstate as it split through truck stops and mini malls and then casinos that sprouted out of the open expanse of the fields. The signs guided me through to Omaha, which I soon discovered was less of a city than a small town that had managed to bud a handful of forty-story buildings in the emptiness of the Midwest.

The ramp into the depths of the city was smooth, the streets clean. Clark's directions led me into this area called the Old Market, which consisted of quaint buildings and cobblestone that reminded me of the Landing back home. I saw a sign for horse-drawn carriage rides and admired the pink and green flowers potted in the gutters of the slanted tin roofs that covered the sidewalks lining the street.

Since I was a bit early, I had expected the area to be packed with people engaged in business lunches and midday dates, but it was nearly deserted. I parked and then walked in the shade past a tobacco shop and a graying man in a top hat and billowing suit sitting above a cane who asked if he could draw my portrait for a few dollars. I thanked him but said no and crossed the street before walking into M's Pub.

I had to hand it to Clark; the restaurant he picked out wasn't bad. I followed the hostess, a brunette in a black skirt, past walls of aged brick painted white and covered in mirrors that made the tight space appear twice the size. Natural lighting warmed the room, and the dark wood floors creaked with the steps of the waitstaff.

Clark was already there, waiting at a table for two near the back. He was thin, a gray-haired rail of a man with a bobbing Adam's apple that was more like a grapefruit than an apple. You can tell a great deal about a man by his handshake. Experts say that when the palm is up, it is an indication of servitude, while a downward-facing palm signifies a personal sense of authority. If the grip is lax, it's associated with weakness. Clark's grip was somewhere in the middle of everything, and he looked at me as though we were old friends as I took my seat. This threw me off and immediately sent me three plays deep into my routine of phony nods and smiles, and I caught myself as I laughed awkwardly at his lame jokes.

I switched gears and asked him for a recommendation from the menu—though, silently, I planned to order the roasted duck salad—and then started chatting him up about the incredibly terrific and amazing restaurant he had chosen.

Clark agreed, the condescension whizzing past his ear, that it was amazing and incredible and terrific. He then pointed to the table where ZZ Top had once sat and how exciting that was, all the while speaking to me in a dialect of nowhereness.

As the lunch progressed, Clark went on and on, querying me about my this and my that, marriage and kids and all the things he expected a red-blooded man of my age to have. I fielded everything as politely as I could, without sounding like a kiss-ass, and I even listened to him go on and on about his children and life in Omaha. I munched on the hard roll that had come with my salad so I didn't have to input anything besides understanding and agreement.

"What's the plan for the day?" I asked as I took the check from our server.

"Well," Clark said, folding his napkin, "I thought I would run us out west so you can see one of our plants for yourself."

"Whatever you think will help the campaign." I grinned, feeding his excitement for this ridiculous adventure. Seven hours in the car to see what? Nothing I couldn't have been emailed or viewed in a cursory Google search. Advertising is about appeal, about developing the appeal for the people, not the advertiser. We'd already been attracted, charmed by the paycheck that would come when the campaign was a success.

Clark insisted we take his SUV, so I plugged the meter and left the Beamer in the Old Market. He talked nonstop about nothing in particular. I learned how many people lived in Omaha, how great of a city it was, and how Bo Pelini was going to lead the Huskers back to glory. I must have asked how far away we were a dozen times, like an excited kid on vacation asking the clichéd line "Are we there yet?" Though I wasn't at all interested in the destination. Rather, I just wanted away from Clark. He was nice enough, sure, but he was small-minded, and his breath reeked of lunch and sinuses, and I was in fucking Nebraska.

The city wasn't much of a city at all. We took a boulevard west, driving for nearly thirty minutes on a four-lane road instead of taking a highway or city interstate, which I assumed they had, though I never saw one. There were restaurants, franchises, everywhere—Chili's and Applebee's and TGI Friday's, Lone Star Steakhouse and Texas Roadhouse, nothing but corporate-dictated menus, flair, and faux vintage crap on the walls, like old license plates and photocopies of movie star memorabilia.

Then the cookie-cutter suburbs rose up before us. They rose but never fell, going on and on, carbon copies of each other sprawling in all directions, their only distinguishing characteristics being the shape of the golf courses they surrounded. We drove on through, navigating the endless mazes of cul-de-sacs, two-car garages, and siding. Siding in every color of the rainbow. So much goddamn siding everywhere. I realized in that moment that this must have been where independent thought went to die, and I knew, listening to how much Clark loved it, that I had the red state blues.

And then, at around 170th Street, we reached the end of the world, and it all just fell off, civilization ending as we found ourselves abruptly in the rural expanse of the West. The highway kept on stretching off until it fell over the empty horizon just as it might have when people thought the world was flat. There was nothing, absolutely nothing, besides cornfields and expanding dusty openings that were treeless, flat, and windswept. I was dumbstruck, silent.

"Amazing, isn't it?" Clark asked as he turned off the four-lane road.

I realized then that he was talking about the ethanol plant, which rose up before us like the Emerald City did for Dorothy and her friends. It was shining white-hot in the midday sun, and as we crossed railroad tracks, I looked up to admire the cylindrical silos and refineries rising out of the middle of a cornfield. No grass. No trees. Just dusty gravel lots surrounding the burnished silver towers and buildings.

Clark flashed an ID to a lazy guard at the front gate and proceeded to drive me through the plant that took up no less than three city blocks. He let me drink it all in, finally shutting up for a moment, and I had to give him credit. It truly was a sight to see. All that power, all that conversion happening right before our eyes. The world moving forward on little bits of corn. That was what I had to sell. I was seeing it, witnessing the possibility, but I knew it was still ridiculous. I knew deep down it would all end in disaster. Clark didn't give two shits about the environment. He drove an Escalade, for Christ's sake.

He stopped at the very edge of the plant and parked. We got out, to our backs the endless nothingness of Nebraska, fluttering stalks of corn, dust, and the West. I put my hands to my hips and stared up at the towers. It was hot, and I squinted, noticing there wasn't a single worker, nobody moving around or running anything.

"Ethanol is just ethyl alcohol, same as the stuff that gets you drunk." Clark chose this as the moment when he would begin his speech, his pitch of inspiration.

"Really?" I knew how to fill in the blanks.

"The compounds are basically the same," he went on. "In fact, bourbon whiskey and ethanol aren't all that different."

I was, surprisingly, intrigued.

"Don't go pouring a fifth of Jack Daniel's into your gas tank now." He laughed, and I could tell the joke was stock, something he had delivered a hundred times. "Seriously, though, the distillation is similar, but we're talking about marketing two very different things."

"Of course."

"We're trying to save the environment." His voice resonated with passion. He believed all of this. "We're hoping to replace fossil fuels and help out the American people by providing a clean, renewable energy source that we create right here at home instead of relying on the Middle East, avoiding all that trouble. American-made biofuels. No more buying oil from terrorists. To tell you the truth, we're behind the curve. The use of ethanol and biofuels is already commonplace in countries like Brazil. It's in our best interest to keep up. To do the right thing for the environment and ourselves. This is our big chance. We need the people of America to know that it is possible to fuel your car, to heat your house with this stuff."

"Is there enough?"

"Enough what?"

"Enough corn to go around. Enough arable land for these crops? What about the market and all that?"

He slapped his thigh and laughed. "Have you seen this state, son? It's a veritable ocean of corn. You may not believe me, but Nebraska used to be an ocean. I mean an actual ocean."

"You're right. I don't believe you."

"I swear it. Back in the Mesozoic, the Western Interior Seaway covered nearly the whole state. There were sharks and those things some people believe old Nessie is."

"A plesiosaur." I had wanted to be a paleontologist as a kid.

"A what?"

"That thing in Loch Ness," I said. "Nessie. They think she is a plesiosaur or something similar."

"Sounds about right." He chuckled. "Now Nebraska is a sea of corn. And unlike fossil fuels, it doesn't take a million years to grow back."

Turning to the west, we stared out at the cornfields. A breeze swayed the green stalks, and they moved together as though an invisible hand of wind passed over them, and it all lilted like the curl of an ocean wave as it approached the shore. These were the amber waves of grain. I thought of the American dream, then the identical houses and unnecessary SUVs running on ethanol. I couldn't decide if the ocean I was staring at was beautiful or another mirage.

"Kind of funny when you think about it," I said after a moment.

"What is?"

"The ways time can change some things, but they inevitably stay the same. An ocean then and an ocean now."

"Oh." He put his hands on his hips and looked out. "Yes, it truly is."

Clark dropped me off at my rental car. It looked like rain, and I was eager to get away. He smiled, genuine and hopeful. I had done my job, and he felt confident that I was the man. I learned long ago that this was my true talent. I never had that great of an imagination or even an understanding of what a great ad campaign was all about. What I did have, though, was that air of confidence. I exuded success and the ability to get the job done. So much so that even if the job got done wrong, clients were still satisfied, thinking that I must have known or understood something they didn't.

But when Clark was gone, I began to wonder about this talent of mine. Ethanol was as outlandishly impossible as the man who was trying to sell it to me. It wasn't going to change the world for the better, but I was going to sell it anyway because I got paid to. After all, I lied for a living, selling the unsellable through witty print and flashy web design. My commodity was interest and bullshit. I made people feel like they had to have something even though, more often than not, I was pushing a product I didn't believe in. If nothing else, it paid the bills, I guess.

I walked over and fired up the 335i. Checking my phone, I noticed I had a voicemail from the office. They were seeking an update, so I dialed but abruptly hung up because I knew I couldn't pretend to care in that moment. I then scrolled down to the J's but closed my phone instead of calling. I was tired of lying and wanted nothing more than to be alone.

CHAPTER 14

August 25, 1986

There are stories of older people who, after decades of marriage, collapse at the loss of their husband or wife. These spouses, soulmates whose lives are so intertwined and codependent that they can't possibly live without their other half, follow the fallen immediately into the dark. You've heard of someone like this, I'm sure. An old woman and her husband who are found still holding hands, the two of them dying only hours, maybe even minutes, apart. Many call this sentimental, even romantic, and they tear up when they learn of a woman who, in essence, gave up on life the moment her husband was buried. It's somehow compelling—for the quixotic among us, at least—that the lives of these elderly people are so inextricably linked that they welcome death because without its embrace there is nothing but desperate loneliness and isolation. Gloria Brown was not one of these people.

My mother claims that the great Gloria Brown was just fine after her husband had collapsed and died of heart failure while mowing the front lawn of their home on North Ballas. Sure, she undoubtedly mourned Mr. Brown's passing and was lonely without him in that big house, but eventually my mother and I arrived, at which point she became as much a parent to me as was possible. She attended Lamaze classes with my mother, read Fitzhugh Dodson's *How to Parent: The Indispensable Guide to Your Child's Formative Years...*, a dingy paperback she had picked up at a garage sale. The two even nested together and babyproofed the house.

Then I was born, named Brett for the strong and independent woman my mother was convinced I was going to be, and Gloria became my nurse so my mother could finish school. She saw to every need of my infant life by feeding me in the middle of the night, pampering my rashes, wiping away my tears, and even rocking me gently through hours of colic. Gloria was there when I first lifted my head at two weeks and stood by, clapping ecstatically, as I crawled at five months. She even cried on the day when, at ten months old, I took my first steps.

I was sleeping and scarcely two years old when Gloria had a stroke. My mother found her on the kitchen floor, a blistery red divot in her left arm where the cigarette had seared her flesh as she convulsed and seized. What happened next, I'll never know. I haven't been able to ask my mother how we left or what became of my first home in Des Peres and my second mother, Gloria. I remember almost nothing and ask nothing of it because my mother can't bring herself to talk of the end.

On the few occasions I've broached the subject, my mother breaks down and refuses to speak. So I have nothing of the woman who cared for me so gently, so sweetly and lovingly, save for the few memories my mother will share and the one faded picture of Gloria helping me blow out my candles on my first birthday. I'm in tears, my face red from bawling, and she looks happy, white-haired and happy with a Karelia Slim burning in her hand, outstretched far from my delicately round, albeit pissed, face. She was only my nurse, a woman who gave us a room to stay in when my mother was desperate, and yet I have caught my mother weeping over that photograph of the older woman standing next to me and proudly smiling. I guess I'll never really comprehend and know that type of bond.

Regardless of how it had happened, we were alone again. My mother and I left to fend for ourselves. My mother took a job selling insurance for a branch of State Farm run by one of her father's golfing buddies. I guess enough time had passed for her to accept a little help. We moved into a house that was too big for the two of us on Sutton Avenue and lived in lonely, loving harmony in the home of my childhood, an English Tudor with a finished attic and a maple tree in the yard.

Over the years that followed, my mother worked through the day while I did what children do in preschool—playing with toy cars and Legos, waiting in line to go down the playground slide, napping on a cot in a dimly lit room while soothing music lulled us collectively to sleep—and then I'd sprint into her arms every day at half past five, when she came strolling into the day care center. In the evenings, it was just the two of us. I'd watch He-Man and the Masters of the Universe, and my mother would read.

As I look back now, my existence, solidified by memories, many of which are slicked in a thicker fog than others, seems to have begun just after my fifth birthday, when my mother taught me how to ride a bike. I scolded her and told her to take her hand off the back of the seat because I could do it myself and didn't need her. Then I cried and screamed at her for letting me fall. I remember losing my grip while climbing the tree in our front yard. After a ten-foot tumble, I landed on the ground with a deafening smack, and the wind rushed from my chest.

And I can see, still clear as day, that late August morning when I was five, weighed down with a backpack and carrying a lunchbox while my mother led me by the hand up the stairs to the front entrance of St. Luke's. She then kissed me and held both of my arms tight so she could lecture me one last time on what I was to do if I got separated from my class. I didn't much listen and was instead elsewhere, caught in a moment that seemed so strange to me then but makes nothing but sense now: the moment when I first laid eyes on Julian. He was crying, his eyes raw and red, his cheeks smeared and puffed, as he struggled to keep himself in the arms of his mother. It was the first day of kindergarten, and she was crying too, pushing him away between saying, "Okay, fine. Just one more hug," over and over again.

CHAPTER 15

THE SPORT OF DROWNING WORMS

I sped away from Omaha, roaring down I-29 on my way back to Julian and Kansas City. Bluffs of sunbaked dirt exposed between cracked and broken trees and bushes that ached for water rose and fell to my left. The Friday afternoon traffic was sparse, save for the semitrucks sailing the seas of America with their cargo.

There were no answers, I thought, consciously trying to convince myself. No solutions to the problem, that baby elephant in the room that Julian, and I in turn through proximity, faced. We had been together, just the two of us, connected by that shared absence and the shame of a father and son baseball game. Life would inevitably change for him now, which would, in turn, alter my life. But would we be better off? His situation was impossible to reverse; there was no going back. He was going to be a father. But what did that even mean? Father? I had never had one, so what did I know? If I were pressed for my opinion, I'm not sure I would have an answer outside the stock response of the patriarch. The protector. The man. Whatever the hell any of that meant.

A blue sign outlined in silver reflectant glinted in the sunlight on my right, the emblem of the ethanol/gasoline blend E85 advertised for the upcoming Phillips 66. I flew by and was reminded of my own problems, those that Julian didn't care to share in. There was time to think, so for the miles and miles that followed, I tried to come up with an answer, a solution. And yet there was this nagging little voice that continued to grow louder and louder as it asked: What the hell was the point? Had I accomplished anything in all of my years writing copy? What difference had I made? What had I truly ever done?

I had to laugh at myself then, the victim of a premature midlife crisis, cannonballing down the interstate in a sports car that screamed of overcompensation. What could be more clichéd than such a man, in such a setting, cogitating the meaning of life? But I couldn't laugh. Not truly. All I managed instead was a sad, desperate sort of laugh, one that resounded with hollow dejection in the solitary bubble of the car and the air conditioning and the whisper of the world going by. There was loneliness all around me, and the laugh reminded me of that. I was alone, moving forward toward death in a pointless existence of consumption and status that made about as much impact as a man arguing politics with an old, deaf dog.

I was speeding, so I eased off the accelerator. The scene around me came back into focus, the tunnel vision of that long interstate drive fading away, and I realized that, up until that moment, I had somehow been immune to the beauty around me. Farmhouses dotted the distance, deep in the open fields where the heat radiated off the ground. I could see a pickup truck off in the distance kicking up the white chalk of an outer gravel road. Despite the miles between us, I was able to make out the blue tarp covering the bed of his truck that flapped erratically in the wind. He was a farmer taking a load of seed or dirt or whatever home, a man like we imagined them, toiling the earth with his hands, a man who created and grew something and lived off what he could make with his brutish, calloused hands as he provided for his family and built what life he could.

Approaching a town—really just an overpass of gas stations, a few homes scattered atop the hillsides, and a McDonald's, always a McDonald's—I found myself a bit bewildered at the notion that people actually lived out in that desolate frontier. And then I saw the cemetery on the hill just past town with a view of the fields and the interstate. The rows of weathered headstones were lined neatly, and all the land between and around them had been scorched, blackened by fire and left to smolder in the heat. Someone had burned the dry grass, torching the land of the dead to leave behind a desolate landscape of soot and charred earth. It was a surreally forsaken scene that stirred something in me. Who could or would burn the land like that? I had heard once that if there wasn't enough water and the grass was dying, it was best to simply burn it, to let the earth start over again. But is that what had happened?

I pressed my foot on the gas pedal again, and as quickly as I had approached the cemetery, I left it to fade behind me. But not its memory. No, that stayed with me. I had seen something, something there was no answer for. I would never know why someone had burned the land. And yet I had this inherent need in me to know, to understand. There was something to tell, a story to create in the void where facts remained unknown. Maybe I could tell and create something to explain it. Maybe I couldn't build a house, toil the land, or wrestle a bull to the ground, but I could create something. Call it story, or fiction, an alternate reality of possibilities. I could spin a yarn, something that might captivate and intrigue. I had done it before. Sure, when I had written before, it had been part of a persona I used to get girls. But I had still written. I had still created. A man can be as much a man creating a story as he can tilling the soil of this good earth. Creation is the mark of accomplishment, and accomplishment the mark of a successful man. At least that made sense in the moment.

After I had tossed the keys of the 335i into the hands of the valet, I walked into the lobby of the Raphael and then immediately ducked from the peripheral of the desk clerk who had given Julian the tickets to the gay rodeo. She was smiling at a guest and nodding idiotically. I wanted nothing to do with her, so I emerged from behind a pillar, my phone to my ear as I feigned a call, then walked briskly through the lobby toward the golden elevators. Of course, she thought we would enjoy a gay rodeo. Two young men, handsome, neat, and well dressed, checking into one hotel room?

As I walked down the fifth-floor hallway, the carpet spongy beneath the soles of my shoes, I asked myself whether I would tell Julian about my day or how I felt. When we were young, I had told him about my writing and even tried to talk to him about the fiction I had written during college, but he had always laughed and mocked me. No, I decided, I wouldn't tell him. I was still far too vulnerable, and it wasn't worth it.

"Hi, honey, I'm home!" I called out, masking any emotions with humor as I entered our hotel room.

It was empty, the room quiet save for the air conditioner resonating with a low-pitched hum, and I figured Julian must have gone down to the pool or out shopping. I had just started to undress when I heard a splash echo from the bathroom, followed by the easily recognizable sound of someone swishing in the bath waters of a filled tub. The door was cracked, and inside the mirror was fogged over with a film of condensation.

"What's up, man?" he said as he looked up at me through a puffy layer of foam. "I must have dozed off in here. How was your meeting?"

"Fine." I was dumbstruck. "What are you doing in here?"

"What does it look like I'm doing?"

I glanced at his toes peeking up through the marshmallow fluff of bubbles and said, "It looks like you're taking a fucking bubble bath. But that can't be right."

"And why's that?"

"Because it's incredibly I don't know... feminine. If there had been candles, I would have never let him hear the end of it.

"So you never take baths?" he asked, and I responded with a concerned shake of my head. "Well, you're missing out." He rolled his shoulders, settling down into the water and closing his eyes as he leaned his head back on the rim of the tub.

I laughed again and left him, returning to the room to continue changing.

"So did you wow the pants off that fucker in Omaha?" Julian was shouting now, refusing to leave the tub though making certain I could still hear him.

"Something like that," I called back.

"That's good. I've got something planned if you aren't in too big of a rush to head home. Something to make up for last night." I heard him rise out of the bath, the water droplets falling off him and making little pinging sounds in the tub as if it were rain falling on a lake. "Should be a damn good time."

"That's what you said about the rodeo, and look how that turned out." I let him feel my cynicism.

"You wanted to find out what it means to be men." He walked out of the bathroom, wrapped tightly in a white terry cloth robe monogrammed with the hotel's logo. "I'm just trying to help out and be a good friend."

"You've never been a good friend," I chided him, plopping onto the bed and crossing my legs, left over right and vice versa, to pull off my socks.

"Aw, don't say that." He passed by to his side of the room and sat down in a firm chocolate-colored smoking chair. "I feel shitty about last night."

"How could you have known it was going to be like that?"

"Either way, I feel like I let you down. I want to make it up to you."

"Don't you just want to go home?" I was feeling a bit tired from the drive and was whining in a way.

"Not at all," he said, cleaning under his nails.

"Oh, that's right. You can't go home."

"You're in a great mood," he said sarcastically, baiting me into a fight. It occurred to me that we were, at times, like an old married couple. "Who pissed in your Cheerios?"

"I'm just tired," I told him.

"Take a nap or something," he fired back. "But don't be a cocksucker."

I leaned back and rested my head on the pile of pillows.

"Come on, let's just do this one thing, then we'll go home if you want. Trust me. It's something you've always wanted to do but have never gotten the chance."

He knew how to be persuasive, that's for sure. Maybe that was the gift that had made him so great at getting himself into trouble.

"Fine," I said, closing my eyes.

"Fine," he mocked, twisting his voice to sound like a nasally Valley girl or snotty high school cheerleader.

When I awoke from a nap, we went out for dinner and drinks at Manifesto, a speakeasy-type of bar in the Crossroads district of Kansas City, which could only be reached by walking down a dark alley between two old warehouses that had been converted into posh lofts and then ringing a bell at the back of the building before being let in. The cooler a place is, the harder it is to find, I guess. Julian had called ahead for reservations, and, as we sat down to dinner, I learned that Julian's surprise was set for the following morning—at dawn, for Christ's sake. One more day in Kansas City seemed like an eternity, but I promised I would go along with it. So after our meal and scarcely enough drinks to tie one on, Julian dragged me back to the hotel, refusing all the while to give me even the slightest of hints.

The room was still pitch-black when I shot out of bed to the blaring alarm. I moved with labored and short, tired steps as I stretched and then set to brew the cheap hotel coffee. As I poured the water into the little plastic machine, I silently cursed Julian for getting me out of bed at this ungodly early hour. Then I began to curse myself because, well, who else did I have to blame? Bringing him here with me had been my idea, and I couldn't help but regret it.

"What should I wear?" I asked, watching Julian dress himself in a thin flannel shirt. He rolled up the sleeves, then pulled on a matching fisherman's stocking cap. His entire outfit was from J.Crew, and all of it bought solely for this mysterious little adventure.

"Something that can get dirty," he said as he examined himself in the mirror. He leaned forward, closer to his reflection, and reached up under the hat to flick out bits of his hair to assure he looked as stylishly rugged in his outerwear as the store had advertised.

"This was supposed to be a business trip," I said. "I don't typically pack for camp when I'm meeting execs for lunch."

"We're not camping."

"You know what I mean," I muttered, rummaging through my suitcase for the outfit I had worn to the rodeo our first night in Kansas City. The khakis and polo were incredibly expensive, as were the boat shoes, but I had little else. I also knew that I would make Julian pay me for them if and when whatever he had planned turned into a disaster.

We checked out, then loaded up the car with our luggage. Julian drove while I sipped coffee from the hotel mug I had stolen. He played morning radio, which featured three hillbilly types arguing politics and making bad jokes with callers. As we rose above the city onto Highway 71, heading north, I watched the rising sun caress the monolithic and mismatched skyline. It was a cool morning, the industrial mess beneath the highway warmed by the dawn.

I asked Julian again what we were doing, to humor him more than anything at this point. He liked to feel in charge and keep things a surprise, so I played along as he took us east on I-70 further into Missouri before turning south to drive into those rural communities that had sprouted just far enough outside of the city to pretend not to be suburbs and instead entitle themselves to some sort of independent identity.

At the intersection of Highway 40 and Woods Chapel Road, Julian pulled off and parked in the gravel lot of a long tin shed, the side of which was painted in massive block letters that read BAIT & TACKLE. The ampersand was accentuated with the tail of a fish, and the whole place looked like we'd need a tetanus booster after shopping there.

"Christ," I said, looking to Julian, who was sporting the mother of all shit-eating grins.

"It's going to be great!" he assured me. "Just great!"

The floor was concrete, the place lit by hanging fluorescent lights that hummed, and it smelled like a veterinarian's office. On the wall were mounted bass, trout, and catfish, twisted and stuffed by a taxidermist so they would still shine in the light and appear as if they were alive and fighting the invisible fisherman trying to reel them in.

Julian paid for everything: the most expensive rods and reels, a tackle box to hold a rainbow of different lures and hooks, and even spray for our lures to attract the fish. He was like a little boy, moving up and down the aisles of stink baits and plastic frogs, poles and reels, sharp hooks and bobbers, and grabbing everything that caught his eye and putting it on the counter in front of the surly cashier who smelled drunk and wore a dingy mesh hat that warned all the ladies out there to "Tell your tits to stop staring at my eyes."

"You boys going to be fishing Blue Springs Lake from the shore?" the sea captain from Jaws asked as he scooped up a pile of earthworms and manure into a Styrofoam cup and then covered it with a plastic lid.

Julian spoke up. "Actually, we have a boat over on Lake Jacomo."

"We do?" I broke in.

"Yes, we certainly do."

It was hard to believe we were only a few miles outside of the city as we crossed over Blue Springs Lake. The water, chopped by boats and the wind, reflected the sky and was luminous and glinting like golden diamonds in the bright sunlight. We continued on, finding ourselves surrounded by vast forests.

Julian sped through, guiding the 335i over the twisting country blacktop until we eventually turned off Woods Chapel and entered Fleming Park. Lake Jacomo Marina opened up before us, the parking lot already filled with cars and pickup trucks, the pavilions and picnic tables crowded with people out early to enjoy their Saturday with family and friends. The lake was filling up with motorboats churning the water and Jet Skis spinning pirouettes like figure skaters while fishermen dropped in lines from their boats or cast from the shores and docks.

We parked and unloaded the car. It stunk like worms, and I complained that we weren't going to get the deposit back. Julian told me he would pay for it, and he walked on ahead toward the dock, his tackle box in one hand and a pole in the other, clearly determined not to let anything ruin this day for us. And in the moment, I admitted to myself that he was right. It might seem strange, but for two city kids without fathers and with delinquent or drunk uncles, there wasn't much guidance when it came to manly outdoor sports. We had waited our whole lives to go fishing. We had talked about it a number of times. Hemingway had loved it. Brad Pitt—who, after films like Fight Club, had evolved into our modern-day John Wayne—had fished in *A River Runs Through It*. There was something beautiful about a group of men in nature, battling the elements and beasts to bring home dinner. I was finally starting to catch some of Julian's excitement.

I carried my brand-new pole, the reel still in plastic, and dragged the cooler along behind me—we being traditionalists who couldn't imagine that fishing could happen without a healthy cache of beer—and I followed Julian onto the maze of boat slips. Most of the boats we passed were covered with tarps and raised out of the water, hoisted by hydraulic or air-filled boat lifts. The floor beneath us bobbed up and down like a trampoline on the wake as a powerboat sped by.

Julian led the way to the end of the docks, and I looked into empty slips where the water shimmered with a film of motor oil and little bits of foam that had broken off the underside of the marina docks and floated with the scum. After passing twenty-footer pleasure craft, pontoons, and professional-looking fishing boats, we finally arrived at our little aluminum dinghy.

Julian had bought it over the phone, paying for it through the same bait and tackle shop we had stocked up at north of the lake, and although he had argued the guy down to only one hundred and fifty dollars, I still thought he had overpaid. It was the length of a canoe, maybe a few feet more, and as wide as a kitchen table. The paint had been chipped down to a blackish metal, and the front of the boat was flattened, bending up out of the water so we could hop the wakes of bigger boats. It was dented all to hell, the metal rippled and bowed as if it had been hammered on.

"You've got to be kidding," I said to Julian as he saddled himself up at the back of the boat, a dingy orange lifejacket that didn't look like it would float tucked under his ass so that he wouldn't have to sit on the hard metal bench seat.

"It's a piece of shit, I know," he said, tinkering with the outboard motor, pretending to know a thing or two about engines. "But the guy said it all runs fine. You've always said you wanted a boat. Now we have one."

"I can't believe you bought this... thing," I said, dropping the cooler down into the middle of the boat, which caused it to bob up and down violently.

"Eh, she isn't so bad," Julian said, grinning as he untied the withered tether that held the stern of the boat to the slip of the dock.

"How are we going to get this home tonight?" I asked, hopping on board.

"Huh... I didn't really think about that."

He then grabbed hold of the cord and tugged on the pull starter of the motor. Smoke billowed out of the engine, black, choking smoke. The motor crackled as it struggled for breath, then finally began idling with a rattling and dull roar. When he twisted the throttle in his hand, the boat lurched forward, scraping against the side of the slip as we shot out, both of us nearly falling overboard as we were jerked from our seats.

Soon we were humming across the open water, bouncing and jumping over the chop like a skipping stone the moment before it topples to the side and sinks below the surface. The lake was brown and crowded with other boaters. Winds blew against my face, and the warm sunshine gleamed onto us as we cut across the water past pear-shaped alcoves. I looked back to Julian, his dark hair riding on the wind like a sail. His smile was so full that I could see all of his perfectly shaped white teeth. I tossed him a beer, then cracked one for myself and drank as we cruised through the sounds and alcoves, splashing over the wakes of other boats, speeding recklessly over logs or sticks floating in the middle of the main channel without a care. After all, who can honestly care about one hundred and fifty dollars when you're having that much fun?

One hour and four beers apiece later, Julian let off the throttle, and we eased to a stop some thirty feet from the bank of a cove on the southernmost tip of the lake. Leaning back, I soaked in the sun and relaxed to the sound of chirping birds and the water lapping up against the side of the little metal jon boat. Julian fumbled about with the fish-finder, a digital screen that mapped out anything that was under the water in low resolution. The thing had cost him almost as much as the boat, but, to my surprise, it worked like a charm, and Julian called me over to see the little fish blips popping up on the screen.

"Okay," I said, taking the plastic off my reel and threading the line through the eyes of the pole. "I've seen this part on the Outdoor Network.

What we're supposed to do is tie a jig on the end of our line, then cast it right next to the bank."

"What's a jig look like?" Julian asked, clinking around through the new tackle box.

"Like something a fish would want to eat."

"What kind of fish?"

"How should I know?" I pictured all the fish I had seen stuffed on the walls of the Bait & Tackle. "Did you ask the guy if there are catfish in these waters?"

He said no.

"Well, that's probably what we're after," I said. "I think they live in the boggy parts of the lake, like a swamp area where there are frogs."

"So should we use these ones?" Julian said, producing two jigs, both rubber and floppy and shaped like little frogs but with barbed hooks sticking out. They looked good to me.

Then came the task of tying them to our fishing lines. I looped the line through the metal eye sticking off the front of the jig and tied it like you would a shoe. It seemed a bit flimsy, so I tied it in a double knot just to be safe.

"Ready?"

"Let's do it," Julian said, standing up uneasily as he straddled the bench seat at the back of the boat. I stood at the front and struggled to keep my balance.

"So all we do is whip the rod over our head and press the little button so it casts as it comes over the top," I said.

"Sounds easy enough," he replied. "On the count of three..."

We counted off, then let it rip. I brought the reel over my head, pressing the button as it came over the top, and felt the jig take off. The weight made the rod bow then instantly straighten as the line snapped where I had tied the knot and the little rubber frog arced high into the air like a home run shot headed for the bleacher seats behind centerfield. I watched as the poor little lure went sailing into the trees and listened to the sounds of it disappearing, crashing into the leafy greenness.

Julian was laughing at me, doubled over as much as he could on the unsteady water. I felt embarrassed for a moment, that was until I noticed that the line coming from the end of his pole dropped straight into the water in front of the boat. He nearly lost his balance laughing but righted himself and decided to take a seat and have another long draft of beer. I picked up mine and drank. It was warming quickly with the sun and tasted awful, so I choked the foam down as quickly as I could and opened another.

"Where is your lure?" Julian asked with tears in his eyes.

"Hooked to a tree bass somewhere high up on that bank," I said, pointing to the woods where my frog had disappeared.

"How did you tie it?" He laughed harder.

"A bow," I admitted, and instantly regretted it. Julian's empty beer can tinked on the floor of the boat, so I threw him another. "How did you tie yours?"

"I don't know," he said, popping the top of his Budweiser. "I just kind of kept making little knots."

"I think doing it right might be a family thing that gets passed down. Like our dads probably had a special way of tying knots for stuff like this."

"Maybe," Julian said. "Or perhaps we shouldn't have quit the Cub Scouts after one week."

"Who gives a shit about merit badges? I just wanted to do the Pinewood Derby. Then they told us how much work it was going to be."

"Yeah, fuck that."

We sat for a moment, thinking back on childhood, I imagine. A hawk circled high up above us, gliding on the wind, the tips of its wings pointing outward as it swooped back and forth.

"What did you do wrong?" I asked him.

"I forgot to hit the little release button," Julian said, holding onto his fishing pole and jabbing it forward into the air like a fencing sword.

He stood up in the boat after I encouraged him to give it another go. Holding the rod firmly with his right hand, he placed his left on the front of it to line things up the way a bowler does before he throws a ball down the lane. Then he came over the top, pressing the button and sending the lure flying through the air, the line following behind it. Maybe we were closer to the shore than those guys on television or we over-muscled it, but Julian's line ended up in nearly the same spot as mine, only his jig was still attached to the fishing pole by some thirty feet of fishing line, the little frog's hooks lodged into a high tree branch.

Julian cursed and started tugging on the pole, which was bending sharply at the middle, looking as if it might break under the strain. The lure refused to budge, and with each pull, we got a little closer to the shore. I have to admit that he tied a damn good knot because the line refused to break until, shouting, "Son of a bitch!" he gave the pole a violent whip, snapping the line that recoiled up close to the end of the fishing rod. He reeled in what was left of his line and tossed the pole onto the floor of the boat, then plopped down for another drink.

I fumbled with my rod and reel to thread the line through the eyes to get it ready for another lure and cast. The smell of the lake rose up on a breeze, and I breathed in deeply, expecting crisp summer air, but instead I was hit with a potpourri of beer and motor oil and bait.

"Maybe we should try fishing in the deeper water," Julian said after a few minutes of quiet drinking. "The guy at the bait and tackle shop told me to snap these weights and a bobber onto our line and then drop them into deep water."

This sounded fine to me, though I couldn't believe that fishing near the bank was really as difficult as we had made it out to be. After all, those guys on the fishing shows I had flipped through were easily over fifty and had beer bellies the size of oil drums.

Julian fired up the little engine and twisted the throttle as he angled the tiller sharply away from the shore. A few gallons of lake water splashed over the side and soaked our feet, and all the cans in the bottom of the boat rode on the brown water, clinking against each other as Julian navigated over the chop.

"It says we're at twenty feet," Julian said as he cut the engine. We idled to a stop in the middle of the lake. He then looked at the fish finder again and gave it a little flick. "Looks like there are some big ones down there!"

We rummaged through the tackle box, carefully pulling out golden hooks with little barbs on them. This time, I looped the line through, taking the care to tie it securely, and then snapped on a bobber and lead sinker. Julian explained that we needed to use the bait, so he pulled the Styrofoam container out and popped the plastic lid off. Earthworms writhed and coiled over the top of each other, tangling in a web of slime and looking like a fistful of lubricated ribbed condoms. I watched Julian's face as the smell of the manure hit him and he stretched out across the boat, twisting away from the container and begging me to take one from him and do it first.

There is this common misconception that all little boys play with worms and dirt and bugs, while little girls playhouse, cooking with their Easy-Bake Ovens and dressing up their dolls. I never ate worms or made mud pies with gravel filling and grass icing as a child. Sure, I had G.I. Joes, and I built them forts and executed full-scale warfare amongst carefully sculpted blankets with cliffs and bunkers and caves, but how far of a cry is that from playing with a Barbie? Their uniforms had to match, and I never lit them on fire with a magnifying glass or blew them up with cherry bombs. I wanted mine to be pristine, their clothes and weapons intact. To be honest, I can't remember enjoying getting dirty as a child.

But I reached out anyway and pinched one of the tails—or heads—of an earthworm between my finger and thumb and then pulled. The rest of it came up from the manure in the Styrofoam cup, springing out like a snapping rubber band. It wriggled against my hand, and as I nearly dropped it, I overcompensated and squeezed out some of the black and brown guts. I nearly retched, but I moved my hands like a surgeon and pierced the earthworm with the hook and line I held in my opposite hand. Julian watched as I impaled the worm and then wound it around itself and skewered it again and again. Dropping the line into the water, I watched the worm sink and then, feeling somewhat satisfied and manly, I opened another beer.

As the line sat in the water, I intently watched the bobber while listening to Julian whine about the smell of the worms and how sticky his hands felt. The minutes passed, and the little red and white bobber scarcely moved. I finished off my beer and reeled the line in, pulling from the water the lifeless and now off-white worm, still run through by the hook but with not so much as a wiggle left in it.

"It's dead," I said, shaking the line up and down until the worm flung off the hook, flipped end over end, and splashed into the water.

"Get another one." Julian was leaning over his line and staring down at the water. "We've got plenty."

And so it went for another three hours. One by one, we scooped the worms from out of the shit and hooked them, smearing our pants and shirts with their bowels before dunking them into the water to let them sink and slowly drown until we reeled them up without so much as a nibble taken from their bodies. The two of us didn't even speak because men don't prattle when attending to serious business.

The heat wouldn't let up, and the lake water in the bottom of the boat began to warm and grow stagnant, the scum and empty beer cans floating together and bumping into our ankles. It might have been the longest, most boring day of my life, but I wasn't going to be the first one to cave. Fishing was what men do, and I wasn't going to let Julian beat me at this game.

"Fuck this," he finally said, the reel of his fishing pole singing as he continuously brought his hand around to pull the line in.

And that's when it happened. Just as his dead worm was about to surface, a fish shot up, taking the whole hook and bait into its mouth. Julian yelled something and stood up, yanking the pole up with startled excitement. The fish came out of the water, still firmly attached to the end of the line, soaring mouth-first at Julian's chest. Julian leaned backward, his body bending and arching like someone doing the limbo. The boat rocked under his weight, and he lost his balance, toppling over the edge and into the water, fully clothed.

The fish landed in the boat on Julian's seat next to the dingy orange lifejacket. It wasn't but six or seven inches long, the body green and slender, slick with water shimmering on the scales. Julian had set the hook so hard that it was popping through the fish's cheek. It blinked, the mouth opening and closing with little o's as it gasped for breath. Then it abruptly whipped its tail and flopped on the metal bottom of the boat, kicking and flying into the air again and over the edge of the boat, where it splashed back down into the water. I leaned over the side of the boat, responding with the reaction time of a glacier, and saw the last glimmer of Julian's fishing pole vanish from sight into the brown depths of Lake Jacomo.

Julian came up out of the water with a spray of lake spewing from his mouth. He looked panicked as he reached out and grabbed the side of the boat. I was still in my seat, a mere spectator who was half drunk and undecided as to whether I sympathized with the fish or my soaked friend. Julian kicked one leg over the side of the boat and pulled himself in. He had lost a shoe. I started to laugh, but he shot me a look like he wanted to strangle me, so I choked it back.

We were silent and sullen while Julian navigated us back to the marina. As the wind dried him and sobered us up, I remembered that Dave Barry had once said, "Fishing is boring, unless you catch an actual fish, and then it is disgusting." He had always seemed like a dweeb, unmanly compared to even Julian and me, but I had to agree. In the end, I was secretly glad the fish had left the boat as quickly as it had arrived. I didn't have the first clue how to clean it, and I suspected that I would have been more likely to lodge the hook into my finger than free it from the fish's mouth.

When we got back to the marina, Julian decided, "To hell with the fucking boat," and so we left it tied to the slip. After all, it wasn't like we were going to tow it behind the BMW all the way back to St. Louis. He abruptly handed the one surviving pole and tackle box to a young boy of nearly twelve who was standing alone on the shore periodically tossing rocks into the water. The boy looked a bit like we had as children, well dressed, his hair neatly groomed by his mother no doubt, and he was equal parts happy and confused when Julian told him that he could keep the fishing gear, that it was a gift.

It wasn't until we were making our way back onto I-70 that either of us bothered to break the silence.

"Well," Julian said, "that didn't go exactly as I pictured."

I played the role of the good sport and smiled as if the thought really did count. To be honest, though, that Saturday had ruined something for me. I may not talk about my father much, but I've always dreamt about what it would have been like had we gone fishing together. For me, that was something pure, something that fathers and sons did together, and it was always good. But that day on the lake showed me a reality I had been too naïve or blind to consider. Fishing was disgusting and boring, and had my father ever taken me, I might have only hated him for it.

"Maybe we should try hunting," Julian said as we peaked the hill outside Columbia, Missouri, the lights of the city orange and warm.

"Like for a deer?"

"We could work up to something that big," he said. "I've read about these outfitters that take care of everything. We could get drunk, sleep in a cabin out in the wilderness like real backwoodsmen, and in the end, all we would have to do is point and shoot. The rest—you know, the skinning of the animal and the meat and all that—is taken care of for you."

"Do you really think that's a good idea?" I couldn't believe he was still after this. In all the years I had known him, he'd never cared to keep doing anything that didn't come easy.

"It beats getting our fingers pricked and handling slimy fish."

I didn't feel like reminding him that we hadn't actually caught any fish and instead feigned as if I were considering it.

"It could make up for all of this crap if we do it right," he said.

"Have you ever even fired a gun?" I asked him.

We hadn't done any of it right. What made him think we were anything but hopeless at this? John Wayne and Clint Eastwood had stunt doubles and fired blanks. Real men might go on safari, but I had read "The Snows of Kilimanjaro" and wasn't going out that way.

"Well, no," he admitted, "but it can't be that hard."

"It can," I said. "And it is. You nearly drowned today. I don't think throwing rifles and more beer into the mix is a good idea. With our luck, we'd probably end up shooting each other."

He laughed, and the idea thankfully died. I leaned my head against the window and closed my eyes as the last bit of tightness from the day drinking faded away and left a vapid exhaustion in its wake. And then I dozed off, lulled to sleep by Julian softly singing along with the Temptations:

Son, Papa was a rollin' stone

Wherever he laid his hat was his home

And when he died, all he left us was alone

CHAPTER 16

April 23, 1980

"I'm pregnant," my mother admitted as she sat on the couch, her hands tucked between her knees, rocking back and forth. The early morning light cut like razorblades through the slits of the plastic blinds, cold as the color of stone.

"Is it mine?" My father stood on the other side of the room, knees locked, back a rigid plank.

She watched the expression on his face as he tilted his head and knew that he must be weighing the possibilities and questioning how he, not much more than a boy himself, could possibly be a father. He was struggling with his second year of college and had no money, no patience for a son. They had only known each other a few months, and growing up, my mother always reminded me that we were never really meant to be a family.

"Of course." She rolled her eyes with equal parts disdain and hurt irritation. But those feelings quickly relented and were replaced by an oppressive hopelessness. She put her hands together as if she were a young child saying her bedtime prayers and then brought them to her face, where the tears began to fall from the corners of her eyes and streak down her cheeks.

"So what do we do now?" he asked.

"I have no idea." She swallowed hard, hoping, wishing, praying that he would cross the vast and barren space between them. She ached for him to hold her, to have the courage to cross that few feet of shag carpet between them and take her in his arms and tell her that everything would be all right.

"Have you thought about getting—?"

"No," she interrupted, not allowing him to say the word he had been avoiding. "I won't. I can't." She shook her head and knew she would never forgive him for even thinking it.

My mother's interruption had made him sweat, and there was no doubt that he was beginning to drown in the reality of it all. She could see the look in his eyes and knew that he felt weighed down, as if he were trying to tread water with a brick tethered to each ankle. And in that moment, the last moment we were a family, all together and in the same room, he simply let out a long sigh.

"I'm so sorry," and then he was off, yanking open the front door and running away down the street.

My mother said she followed him to the door and looked out to watch him sprint away wearing nothing but a pair of boxer shorts and a t-shirt, his bare feet clapping against the sidewalk. He left behind his wallet and his keys and a drawer full of clothes, and they, along with the few stories my mother has told me, are all I have left of him.

CHAPTER 17

FATHER'S DAY

I was able to sleep nearly the entire way back home to St. Louis, but it was a restless sleep, a limbo of dreamlessness. For two hours or more, I had drifted somewhere between oblivion and dim half-sleep, as if I were catatonic. Even when Julian exited to find a gas station and fill up the BMW, I continued to sleep, albeit restlessly, warmed by the white lights that buzzed like insects in the summer night. It wasn't until we turned south off I-70, merging into the five lanes of I-270, that I woke, the taste of sleep heavy on the back of my tongue.

"Almost home," I said involuntarily, hunching my shoulders and yawning.

The road can be long for someone with nothing to think about, and I awoke with the hope that Julian, having chauffeured me across the state, had used the time to think things over. For all I know, he'd thought of nothing, but I can't recall any other time when he had ever let me sleep. Julian was a friend, yes, a best friend, but he was far from selfless. When we were boys spending the night at each other's house to build basement forts out of sheets, he would always poke me in the ribs with his thumb to keep me awake when he couldn't sleep. And that habit continued and spread through adulthood. He was always dropping by uninvited to bug me or calling at ungodly hours to drag me out of bed for a variety of invented reasons. I had always pretended that this all bothered me, of course, but in truth it was comforting to go through life with a kind of partner. For two people who seemingly never want to be with any one woman for very long, we both had trouble being alone.

But in that moment when he exited onto Clayton Road, the look on his face revealed nothing. His countenance was stoic, eyeing the road ahead without even a glimmer of wandering thought, as if he had just been focused on the road and had let me sleep because he knew I was tired. I knew that couldn't be the case, though, and that there must have been something there, something that had occupied his mind and kept him from waking me with a joke or smacking me so I could enjoy one of his farts with him.

It was maybe eight when we pulled into his driveway. Seventy-two hours, and we were back where we had started. The plan for manly adventures, the rodeo, the bars and the women, the ocean of corn, the boat and the worms, was becoming an unpleasant and distant memory. All I could think of was sleep.

"Hard to believe it's only Saturday," Julian said, tugging at his duffle bag, which was snagged on something in the trunk.

"We could have stayed another night," I said, and immediately wanted to take it back. Three days of close-quartered living must be the breaking point for even the greatest of friendships. More than that and we might have killed each other, especially considering the disastrous failings of our whole adventure into the world of masculinity.

"I just mean it's Saturday night," he said. "Feels like we might be wasting one of our favorite nights of the week."

"I'm pretty beat." It was the truth.

He shrugged, agreeing silently that, even though it was early, we didn't really have it in us. I don't feel old, but even I have to admit that I can't do some things the way I used to. A day of drinking in the hot sun takes it out of you.

I looked up at his house as he closed the trunk. Both stories were dark, uninviting. It might as well have been a stranger's home, one like the thousands I had passed driving through the city and suburbs. A home, even the home of your friend, becomes a bit like your own because it has character, it has a story, and you're connected to it. But on that evening, Julian's house in Frontenac wasn't a home. It was a bunker, an escape from his problems and responsibilities. Maybe that was why our adventures that weekend had gone so sour. They hadn't been undertaken with earnest but were rather a side note to a weekend meant as an escape, a couple of days for us to get away from that baby elephant that had been chasing us about the room.

"Brett," Julian started, looking down at his feet and shuffling them on the drive before turning back to me. There was something strange resonating in his voice. It was as if something were keeping him from going on, and I realized, then, that it was self-consciousness. But that couldn't be the case. Julian was never self-conscious, at least not outwardly. He was overly confident to a fault. And yet I could tell there was something wrong, something that was eating at him.

I met his eyes and nodded, letting him know I was there for him.

"You know how sometimes a lie, after it's told enough times, can become true in its own way?" Julian had never talked this way, but I didn't say anything. I continued on with my nods, eager to hear it all. "Over these past few months, I've said things about it not being mine, or that she was trying to trap me, but I never really believed any of it. The night that I think it all happened... I can't get it out of my head. It's like a bad dream that I can't seem to shake. We had fucked so many times, countless times, but that night we were aggressively drunk."

He paused as a car drove by. It was night, but the million streetlights of the city lit the sky with a dull orange glow that eclipsed the stars.

"I never wear condoms," he continued. "I know it's stupid, but I just hate them. I always have, even when we were teenagers. It just doesn't feel real with one on. I might as well be fucking one of those gloves you wear when you're doing the dishes."

I tried not to laugh, but this is the way men talk. We avoid our feelings, sidestepping them with jokes, breaking up the seriousness with vulgarity.

"We were so damn drunk, and I'm not sure if I came in her or not, but I might have," he said, and I couldn't tell if he was angry or fighting tears. Maybe it was both. "I must have."

"What are you trying to say, Julian?"

He looked me in the eyes, those brown eyes black in the night, like staring into a well, the darkness consuming the depths after a few feet. There was so much pain, but I needed to hear the truth from him.

"I'm saying that it could be mine." Julian had finally said it. "The kid's mine."

There was silence, broken only by cicadas and crickets and the hum of the streetlight at the end of his driveway. It might as well have been the moon, full and white, shining down on us like a spotlight on a bare stage.

"What are you going to do?" I asked after what must have been only minutes but seemed like an eternity, eons to think about what he had admitted.

Julian shrugged. "I don't know," he said with the coldness that consumes honesty in men. "The same thing I've been doing, I guess."

I had never hit him or anyone before, never punched another man in the face. But in that moment, I wanted to knock out his perfect white teeth and beat some sense into him. I stared at him and clenched my jaw and rapped my knuckles against my thigh. In the end, though, I said nothing because that's what men do. We don't share our feelings or opinions, and it wasn't my place to interfere. That baby was his, and if he wanted to abandon it, then I guess he had every right to do so.

"Sorry to get so deep after a good time," he said, smiling now.

"Forget about it," I said, walking over to him.

"You had fun, right, Brett?"

"Of course," I said as I wrapped him in a hug and patted his back.

"Good."

It was always most important to him that we had fun. A good time outweighed all the consequences.

"I'll call you tomorrow," I lied.

I watched him walk up the driveway to his front door, the duffle bag draped over his shoulder and his suitcases rolling behind him. Like a woman, he always packed too much. I exhaled deeply, wanting to say so much but lacking any courage.

The car rental depot was only a mile or so from my house in the Central West End, but by the time I dropped off the BMW and they had given me a ride home, it was nearly ten o'clock. I couldn't remember spending a Saturday night at home. When people "grow up," when they give up on having a good time to get fat and take care of their children, the weekend is the first thing to go. One by one, my old friends had "settled down," as they called it, had kids, and lost their Friday and Saturday nights. I felt sorry for them, sitting at home on the couch watching television because they couldn't go out. I worried that I might be turning into them, but as I plopped onto the couch and started flipping through the channels, I told myself that it couldn't be so because it didn't feel like Saturday.

There was nothing on, and I stank like fish bait, so I took a shower and crawled between the sheets, where I could hear a group of twentysomethings, a few years younger than me, hollering and laughing drunkenly, the girls' heels clicking on the pavement as they piled into a taxi. For a moment, I felt something like an outcast, as if I was missing out on something. But then I shrugged it off, and once they had gone, fell into a much-needed sleep.

I overslept, waking at nearly ten o'clock on Sunday morning, cotton-mouthed and aching, then pulled myself out of bed and left it unmade. The carpet beneath my feet was like walking on a sponge, and I imagined myself bouncing groggily as though I'd been hibernating for twelve years instead of twelve hours.

After a shower, I dressed, pulling a Golden Fleece polo from Brooks Brothers over my head, then tousled my wet hair, shaking it loose. The shirt was light blue with a navy collar and a broad matching stripe that went across my chest, the bottom of which was hanging over the top of my boxer shorts. The Brooks Brothers logo, a fatted sheep suspended by a bow, was red and finely stitched on my left pectoral. I looked at myself in the mirror above my long bedroom dresser and could see that I needed a shave but figured it was Sunday, so what the hell.

It was then, as I leaned forward into the mirror for a closer look, that I noticed something. The hairs on my face were not the flaxen color I had known my whole life, not all of them at least. There was a hoary shade streaking across my cheek, the lightest silvery hint to my facial hair. It had been two days since I had last had a shave, and that was enough to show the truth: I was going gray. A number of times I had plucked a stray white hair from my fair head. Most were coming in above my ears, and I would promptly pull them out, follicle and all, with a pair of tweezers. But this was different; my face couldn't easily be dyed or plucked. I never grew a beard or a mustache, but that was beside the point. Now I could never grow one.

I had been so desperate to first grow facial hair as a boy, armpit hair too. It felt like the other boys developed all that before me, and it made me self-conscious, like less of a man. I would shave, streaking my mother's razor across my bald, boyish face, accidentally drawing blood from my philtrum when I would press too hard or catch the top of my lip. All I had wanted back then was to become a man as quickly as possible, to keep up with the other boys whose hair was sprouting here and there. I was behind all of them, maturing slowly, and then there I stood, not yet thirty and still staring into my prematurely graying face.

After pulling on my khaki shorts and slipping into a pair of leather sandals, I styled my hair and headed out into the living room, where there was nothing to do but sit. I passed the time, flipping through the channels. There wasn't a game on, not like it would have mattered considering how far out of contention the Cardinals were.

I considered, as I aimlessly changed channels, the handful of women I could call, the ones in my phone that I kept in just enough contact with to make something happen at the drop of a hat. One in every port is what they—and my mother—call it, but mine were scattered throughout the same metropolitan area, a practice that would allow me, after a bit of posturing and small talk, to set up a day date in Forest Park or the zoo, or even dinner somewhere, always before finishing the night in my apartment. But the setup was always so tedious. I would have to go through calling each of them. Some wouldn't answer, and out of the ones who did, I would be stuck catching up for twenty minutes, even if they weren't interested in spending the day and night with me. They would blather on—inane chatter being the inalienable trait all women share—and then I might discover they were in a new relationship, which, of course, I would have to hear about to continue the charade of friendship. And then, when the conversation was over, I would hang up and delete them from my phone soon after. It didn't seem worth all of that hassle simply to not be alone, to get a little.

I thought of Julian. There was no way I could call him. What he had told me the night before was something to take in, an admission I had to think about. I almost couldn't forgive him for what he had done to us. I had hated being on the run, hiding out from this woman. That night she found us at the Landing was enough to scare any man, especially one who knew he was wrong. A woman scorned is a dangerous thing, and I knew Julian couldn't run forever, though he would likely try, and there might be big trouble after the kid was born. What the hell was Julian going to do about child support? I wondered if it was a percentage of his income or if it was a set monthly fee. No matter. Whatever it was amounted to a high price for being too stupid to wear a rubber.

And as though all of this wasn't enough, a television commercial, pixels radiating, caught my eye, and I found myself staring at an advertisement for cheap neckties, grill sets, and power drills, all accompanied by an animation of balloons and confetti and "Father's Day Sale" that wrapped up the whole spectacle. Call it astrology or karma or any other voodoo, but there was something in the stars, something written, dictating that my day would be shit. The irony is that it was actually written, plastered across the television in bold type, screaming at me: Father's Day! The gods couldn't be any more obvious... they hated me.

I couldn't leave the house now. At least in my home I was safe. But outside I would be subjecting myself to all the happy bastards grilling in their yards, stinking up the fresh summer air with the sweet smell of barbecue. What was Father's Day anyway but a holiday designed to share misery, to spread umbrage and silent, smiling annoyance to all? I don't say any of this as a cynic. As one of the fatherless, I am but an unbiased, impartial observer to the madness of those who voluntarily submit to a day that, like most holidays, brings about nothing but burden.

The day is lauded as this celebration of fatherhood, but despite the best of intentions, it remains like Christmas and Thanksgiving and all the others: another day we have to go out and buy things people don't need. Each year, as June approaches and the first three weeks of the month pass, the commercials and advertisements and sales take over, and their annual resurgence serves as little more than a grating reminder to sons and daughters alike that it's time again to celebrate dear old Dad, to buy him a present and make plans to spend their special Sunday with family. Another Sunday crossed off the calendar and wasted. Make no mistake, these sons and daughters do indeed harbor a silent antipathy because fathers are meant for resentment. They are men, after all, made in the image of God and designed to be loved but not known, feared but not understood. Fathers, like God, are dictators, and it cannot be forgotten that you can't have a dictator without the man, the dick, behind it, the essential root of the title itself who is the powerful feudal lord that rules his household with an iron fist.

And these men, these fathers, are given a Sunday, a day appropriately shared with the God with whom they mirror so many immutable character traits, but what of them? Do they feel the appropriate scorn of a wasted day even though they are the center of the celebration? Of course they do! Because, after all, they have fathers of their own.

But what's worse, what's more callous still, is that not everyone has a father, and for those without, the day is merely a cruel reminder of this absence. All of these people at their barbecues, buying and wrapping gifts for some invented waste of a holiday, are the lucky ones, the blessed ones who are allowed the convenience of resentment for the man responsible for their existence. I, on the other hand, could only dream of resentment because the man who was my father did not exist.

In truth, I hated those who had fathers, those who were allowed the resentment, the inconvenience of having to buy gifts for undeserving men and then waste a Sunday each June with family. I asked myself, then, would the significance, would the pain this holiday induced change for me if and when I ever had children? Or would my presence in their life, the power drills and macramé gifts and hand-scrawled cards in crayon they would give me, merely remind me of the absence in my own life? My own fatherlessness? And then, in that moment, even though the commercial for the Father's Day sale had long since passed, I clicked off the television and stared into the black screen as I engaged in that all-too-familiar pastime of feeling sorry for myself.

I was now enveloped in a deaf blanket of loneliness, the afternoon sunlight breaching the curtains to brighten the bland white walls and reflect in the television the scene before it: an uncluttered coffee table, my couch, and the poor soul sitting and looking forward into his own dark reflection. There I was, a young (though not that young) and handsome (though not that handsome) man who was, in truth, utterly alone and empty. I felt it then, the truth that I was an island, and I knew that it had always been that way.

There are two types of memories: those we can't take with us and those we wish we couldn't. The half-memories, the ones we can't seem to carry whole, exist as if they were dreams, something seen from afar, things that happened to us or things that we had, but we can remember them only from the outside, a snapshot in time, as if watching a grainy home movie of ourselves. They're typically happy, like the memory of our first bike, perhaps, or that one special Christmas morning when we got everything we asked for and more. When there is enough distance, enough time, all we're left with is a collage of broken and half-pictured events, no matter how we strain to keep all the pieces together. Then there are the other sort of memories, the ones we pretend never existed in the first place, the bad dreams we wish would simply fade away. And it was, of course, the latter sort that crept up and haunted me, as I sat on the couch and stared at my reflection in the television, on that Father's Day after Julian had told me Maria's unborn child was his.

I'm not sure why, but I have always hated Sundays. Even now, a deep pit of loneliness always accompanies the end of the week. I remember it was bedtime on a Sunday when I was nine, and I was hiding in our house on Sutton Avenue. I was lying in the narrow space between my bed and the wall. There was a dusty itch to the carpet there, a smell that tickled my nose, but it was dark in that gap where I had shoved myself and then pulled pillows over me. With the outside world blocked out, I was free to cry, and I recall that each whimper and sob was accompanied by a sense of shame.

"I want to go home," I said to my mother when she finally pulled the pillows off and asked what I was doing crying all alone like that.

"But you are home, Brett," she explained softly.

Then I told her the truth, the real reason I was hiding. I admitted to my mother that this home, this place she had worked so hard to build for us, had never felt like home to me and that I was alone, empty, and that there was nothing she could do to change that, and that she should just leave me be.

I can remember even now how she said nothing. She didn't scold me or point out the absurdity. No, she was too hurt for that. Instead, it was as if the entire world drained from her face. My mother knew, more than most, really, that every man is an island unto himself. But in that moment, she couldn't help but cover her face and run away weeping because I had cut her so deeply.

CHAPTER 18

PERIODIC TESTOSTERONAL FLUCTUATION CYCLE

It is a little-known fact that men get their period too. We may not bleed or need pads, but we have a lot of the symptoms, regular as clockwork. It may seem farfetched, but you can't fight the science.

The female hormonal cycle of primates is highly evolved, relying on precise chemistry and involving uteri and yolk-filled cytoplasm, not to mention those lady bits and pieces that men have not. Unlike men's bodies, women's bodies, when pregnancy doesn't occur or when women pick up Plan B at the local free clinic, go through a series of changes, the start of which is the drop of an egg that is expelled from the body along with the uterine lining. What follows is a painful series of back pains, bloating, headaches, nausea, and, of course, cramps so intense that many women fall down in tears despite a questionably higher tolerance for pain.

This all results in irrationality, mood swings, bitchiness, etc., all of which I, a male raised by a single woman, unfortunately know firsthand. And even though my mother, having dropped her last egg and gone through what she refers to as the "change of life," has since apologized to me for the monthly torment I was forced to endure, the emotional scars from, say, being backhanded for saying her perfume was a teensy bit strong remain.

And yet, men share a similar torture. Impossible? Why? After all, we're cut from the exact same cloth. The blueprint of man is inherently female. In fact, in gestation, we're all female until the second month, when the expression of a single gene, the Y chromosome, is sprinkled into the mix. That little Y, as pathetically unphallic as it might be, has given us Plato, Hitler, Shakespeare, Napoleon, Beethoven. Without that Y, our giggle berries would have been ovaries, the cock a clit, our ability to drive a car properly or dunk a basketball nonexistent. And since we share these genetic commonalities—think of the analogous nipples on men if you're still not convinced this is the case—then why is it so far-fetched that we cocksmen share in the woman's hormonal cycles?

Sanctorius of Padua, some four hundred years ago, was the first to propose the idea of the male monthly cycle. Way back in the seventeenth century, this Italian physician weighed himself, everything he ate and drank, and everything he subsequently expelled and discovered that men's bodies undergo a monthly cycle that, at its peak, is marked not only by weight gain but also by lethargy and inexplicable irritation.

Granted, this cycle of marked fluctuations in male testosterone levels is in no way comparable to the shift women undergo, but that isn't to say we don't still have a cycle. Dubbed irritable male syndrome—IMS for short—after the term coined for the drop in testosterone levels among male mammals toward the end of mating season, this shifting hormonal cycle occurs in all men and is marked by physiological and chemical changes that affect us sexually and emotionally. We become angry, anxious, hypersensitive, and irritable, and experience hot flashes and headaches and stomach cramps, among other things. Worst of all, this IMS can cause a lack of arousal and even sexual dysfunction.

But my point in all of this isn't to stir up some debate to level the playing field between the suffering of men and women. Rather it's to point out that it was certainly no coincidence that, on the day I finally confronted Julian about Maria and the baby, I awoke to find myself some five pounds heavier than normal, bloated, with a headache.

It was the Tuesday following Father's Day. I hadn't eaten anything out of the ordinary, and the night before had been calm. I spent the night planted on the couch in front of an away game, putting the finishing touches on the campaign for E-First. What I had devised was aimed at convincing people that using America's corn surplus for fuel would be good for both the national economy and the environment.

The audiovisual, one that we would post on the new E-First website and run in a variety of outlets, followed a turtle across a busy highway, the traffic narrowly missing him as it speeds by until a little girl in one of the cars makes her father pull over to rescue it. Then, setting the turtle down in a beautiful cornfield, the child tells the audience in a voiceover just how, if we use clean fuel grown and manufactured right here in the good ol' USA, we can make the world a better place. It's all done in live action, which is amazing because the little turtle actually looks like he's coughing when the digital smog hits his face. You probably saw the commercial version, a thirty-second spot that was broadcast in most states and closed with E-First's company logo and information for a "better tomorrow."

To be honest, I stole the whole "turtle crossing the busy road" thing from Steinbeck, but it didn't matter. Nobody reads anymore, so no harm, no foul. The campaign was hard to resist, as was I, standing in my charcoal with bold rope stripe Gianni Manzoni suit with a paisley tie and solid pocket square to pitch everything to my higher-ups and Clark. As I took my seat, smiling and basking in their approval, I was conscious of my ability to act because, while I outwardly portrayed strength, intelligence, and advertising genius, inside I was burning alive, and my stomach was twisting itself into knots.

Once the meeting adjourned, I rushed back to my office to phone Julian so we could celebrate with a long happy hour and dinner. It was, you could say, a tradition of ours because each time an ad is completed and sold, I'm washed with relief to have the lie finally off my shoulders. Unlike your run-of-the-mill, everyday lies that linger in memory and remain a piece of their creator, I relinquish all ownership of my advertisements the moment I turn them over to my clients. This abandonment is so strong, so complete that when I see them on television or in print, I feel as if a stranger might have conceived them, which, in the end, is partially true. But for some reason, even as I was dialing Julian's number and telling him to meet me at Café Napoli, I couldn't seem to shake how hollow my victory had been and how unsettled by the burden I remained.

It was damn hot out, and I could feel the sweat causing my suit to bunch on my back as I made my way into the restaurant. I hated that, sweating when I was well dressed. The product in my hair was running down onto my forehead, and I touched it with my fingertips.

"You look like shit," Julian said to me when I found him in the crowded restaurant. He was sitting comfortably in a leather loveseat to the left of the bar, legs crossed and sipping on what looked like a mojito, the glass sweating, the mint green and refreshing.

"No, no, don't get up." I fell into the chair opposite him and called him a prick under my breath.

A crowd continued to fill the hip martini bar and restaurant, lining the leather bench seats and tables. Happy hour was in full swing, and since there wouldn't be any available tables, it was only natural to sit and drink, getting tighter and tighter as the bar became so crowded that we would have to shout to hear our thoughts on such philosophical subjects as what kind of suit we planned to buy next or the approximate size of a pair of faintly glimpsed tits.

I can't always handle the crowds, especially when I'm feeling as uncomfortable as I certainly was on that afternoon. It felt as if everyone around us was closing in, looking at us and staring. I squirmed, needing to get away, to escape to the bathroom maybe and compose myself. To fix my hair, for Christ's sake! The first sips of my drink weren't doing me any good. Where did Julian get off telling me I looked like shit, that posh son of a bitch?

"So I got a haircut today." He started the way people often do when they begin a story. But whenever he did this, the story never went any further. It was merely an intro, a way of centering the focus of the conversation on his favorite subject: Julian.

"It looks good," I said, and it truly did. The tresses, black and longer, were styled away from his face, a few soft curls tucked behind his ears.

"Yeah," he went on. "They raised the price again."

"Did you go to Cynthia?" We went to the same stylist at Preston's in Clayton. Had for years.

"Of course." He watched a young server pass by, eying her bare, taut legs hungrily. "It's over fifty now for a cut and style."

"Christ." I didn't want to get into how ridiculous it was to pay for a full cut when he got only a trim again. "At least you look good. That's what really matters."

He smiled, and we raised our glasses to each other and then drank. The server with the long legs, bare and defined between her skirt and black flats, walked by again.

"You get a look at that?"

"Of course I did," I said, loving her because Julian did and hating him because he had a better chance of having her at that moment.

"One of us should go talk to her."

"She's working," I said, "and barely twenty. The last thing she wants is a couple of assholes creeping on her."

"A bit jaded, are we?" he replied. "What's wrong? The fairer sex getting you down?"

"I haven't gotten up, down, anything for nearly a month now," I admitted reluctantly.

"No worries, my friend," Julian said, that cocky turn to his smile dimpling his cheek. "We'll get your bone smooched tonight if it kills us."

We ordered another round and sat drinking amidst the ambient noise of ice cubes clinking against glass and the collective chatter of twenty-five people listening to themselves talk while the other twenty-five pretended to listen.

"You'll never guess who tracked me down, yet again," Julian broke in, crushing an ice cube between his back teeth.

He didn't need to tell me the story. I already knew it, but of course I stupidly asked who anyway.

"Maria." It's funny how we can be programmed to both laugh and fear a proper noun the moment we hear it. "She fucking got me at the grocery store." He always laughed at his own stories, which you might be surprised to learn wasn't as annoying as it might seem. Whenever Julian did it, you laughed along because it was charming and you were sharing something. But this time, I couldn't laugh because it just wasn't funny anymore. "I was at Schnucks, pushing my cart down the produce section and stopping to molest a couple of C-sized grapefruits to see if they were ripe," he went on. "You know, minding my own business. And then, out of the corner of my eye, I spot her hiding behind a pyramid of bananas."

He paused, expecting me to be on the edge of my seat and laughing. I knew I was supposed to say, "What did you do, Julian?" or "Holy shit, man. How did you get out of there?" but instead remained silent.

"What's wrong?" Julian asked, his self-consciousness peeking through at me. "Don't you want to hear the rest of the story?"

"Not particularly."

"Why the hell not?" he asked. "You're acting like a real whiny bitch today."

"I'm not acting like anything," I shot back. "I just don't want to hear another one of these stories, is all."

"Oh, got it," he scoffed. "What would you like to talk about then?"

"That woman is carrying your fucking baby, Julian. Your son, maybe."

"Oh, what the fuck!"

"Don't interrupt me," I said.

"Don't talk down to me."

"I'm not," I said, my voice trembling. "I just can't stand this shit anymore. What if your father hadn't cared if you existed, Julian?"

"But he did."

"Well, mine didn't," I said, squeezing my fist so tightly around my glass of beer that I thought it might shatter.

"So that's what this is about," he said, actually laughing aloud in my face.

"No, you pompous prick!" I shouted as I leapt out of my chair and took him by the shirt, pulling him up so we were up close, face to face, some six inches apart, where he could feel my breath and spit. "This is about you and your baby. You're going to be a father. You have a responsibility to that baby. It isn't about you anymore. Don't you see that? That child is yours, and you have to be a fucking man!"

"Let go of me," he gasped as I tightened my grip on his collar. People were staring at us now, but I didn't care.

"You're my brother, Julian," I told him. "My best friend. But so help me God, if you don't do something to make this right, I'll knock your teeth down your fucking throat. It's time for you to start acting like a man, or I will never fucking forgive you."

And with that, letting him fall back into his chair, I straightened my tie and, ignoring all the gawkers, pulled some twenties out of my wallet and tossed them on the table the way mobsters like De Niro in *Goodfellas* or James Caan at the beginning of *The Godfather* do. Then, I stormed out and it felt great.

CHAPTER 19

October 27, 2004

I was in love once, and like most loves, it ended badly. I remember the date because that was the day the Cardinals lost the World Series to Boston. People rarely remember who came in second, but I can't forget the last time we ever spoke, that Wednesday evening when I asked her to forgive me. When she refused, I slammed down the phone. I'd convinced myself that the Cardinals losing was a sign, a reaffirmation that she and I were never meant to be. So while much of the world celebrated a miracle run and the end of sports' greatest curse, I sat alone on my couch, drinking and watching the fireworks erupt in the night sky above the hugging players that cried and told reporters they were going to Disney World. And then, turning off the television, I sat in the dark and contemplated what I had done.

The way we'd met wasn't exactly romantic, but not much is these days. It seems like all the good love stories are taken, saturated by romantic comedies and sitcoms. There's nothing original about a love story anymore, not the way the world works nowadays, and that's why I met Kerrie at the gym on Union in the Central West End called St. Louis Workout.

There are always so many women at the gym, and Julian and I had picked that spot because the clientele was a talent pool filled with girls our age and younger. The two of us, like almost everyone in America, didn't work out for sport or health or to train for anything. No, we did it for vanity. The countless mirrors in gyms, after all, are there for men like us, men who can't help staring at how our muscles tense as we squat-thrust or do cardio, working for those long, lean muscles instead of bulk. There were signs around the fitness club, motivational posters that quoted Vince Lombardi, that were calculated to drive us to all play like champions. But we weren't playing for anything. Nobody was obese or pushing themselves so they could be the best on the football field. You didn't work out if you didn't look good doing it. It was all about sweat and sex and pheromones.

But Kerrie was different. While everyone else was working glutes for looks, she was running for endurance. I learned later that she had played basketball in college and could never break the habit of training. She wasn't interested in how she looked doing it, or the unspoken sexual barriers that fell to the wayside when you put on spandex shorts and a sports bra and started sharing sweat with people of the opposite sex. If only Julian had known that before he hit on her.

I watched as he sidled up, checked her over from head to toe, and then made his move. She was at the water fountain, panting and wiping the sweat from her brow, and I saw her blush when he complimented her form or something sleazy like that. But she turned out to be no shrinking violet because I overheard her ask him if he'd chosen his ridiculous workout getup of short shorts, cutoff shirt, and gloves the night before to impress all the little coeds. He flushed with embarrassment when she said that, something I hadn't seen before, and I liked her immediately.

Over the weeks, I nodded and smiled when I saw her, until one day we got to talking. I was looking up at a mounted television, reading the subtitles of a Baseball Tonight replay between sets, when she came over to watch the show. It was the off-season, and they were covering the Cardinals' trades and pickups and the upcoming spring training camps in Florida. After a moment, she started talking about how pitching wins championships and explained why we had a shot to win it all this year. I was shocked, in a way, because she actually knew more about the game than I did.

I took her out, and it was different because I didn't just want to nail her. She made me laugh, and we talked, actually talked. There were no games, no feigning of interest just to get into my bed or hers. I mean, eventually we got there, but it wasn't about that. Something was changing. I looked forward to seeing her, enjoying the time we spent together rather than simply going through the motions.

Those ten months of my life were special. Kerrie had a way about her. She was beautiful, with full lips and great skin, but it was more than that. Her personality was warm, her laugh sweet and infectious. And even though she had rejected him, Julian liked her too, although he would never come right out and admit it. It was in the fall when I decided I was going to ask her to move in with me. I wanted to take the next big step, one I had never considered before, one toward a future.

"You're too young," Julian had said, crossing his legs, leaning back in our booth at Café Eau in the Chase Park Plaza. We were sitting in the darkness of the New York glam décor, drinking and not dining because nobody but tourists ate there.

"Too young?" I laughed, leaning forward. "I'm almost twenty-four."

The ice in my glass clinked against the sides of the tumbler. Julian had been on a Rat Pack kick and had learned that Chivas Regal was the favorite of Frank Sinatra's, which was the catalyst for our "Scotch phase," a hobby that lasted almost six months and cost God knows how much money. We sat in dark places, trying countless brands, using words like quaffable and discussing the peaty notes of the Scotches from Islay and the superiority of Speysides. We went to tastings and tried to be connoisseurs, but it didn't quite take. To be honest, I had trouble telling the difference even between blends and single malts, but didn't say anything. It looked cool and got me tight, which was all that really mattered.

Julian went on. "It's the prime of our lives, and you're going to throw it all away on some girl?"

"How does it even affect you? Has my being with her gotten you any less?"

"It will be different." Julian shook his head. "You will change. We won't be able to go out like we do. You'll have to be with just her too."

"I have been with just her."

"Really?"

"Really," I was able to say with honesty. "Since she and I first got together."

"But I've seen you talking to women, playing wingman for me."

"I'm usually talking about her." I laughed. "Women love that crap."

"Well, I guess I can't complain because it has been working," Julian said, shrugging. "But that's not the point. I just think it's a bad idea. I think you're going to fuck everything up when we're still young. Get married when you're old, like when you're thirty-five or something."

"I've already given her a key," I said, smiling up at him.

My mother wasn't much better when I told her. I was over at the old house, the one on Sutton, for our weekly dinner. Every Sunday I had to be there, or I would never hear the end of it. If there had been a game or it was football season, I often went drunk, but she didn't care. What mattered was that I was there to fill the emptiness of the house.

"Sacher-Masoch wrote that a woman's character is her lack of character," she said as we shared a bottle of wine after dinner, instantly reminding me why I had stopped talking to her about these sorts of things in high school. My father's abandoning us had done something to her, surely, but to this day, I can't explain how she grew to distrust women as well as men.

"I know, Mother," I said in a son's typical exasperated tone. "You made me read it twice, remember?"

She smiled. Nothing about our kitchen had been changed since the mid-eighties. I sat there, watching the Quasar microwave oven clock as it told me, minute by minute, how badly I didn't want to be there.

"You care about this woman, Brett?" she said, lighting a cigarette.

"Of course I do, Mom." I set my glass down. "I love her."

"You honestly think, with over six billion people in this world, half of them being women, that this one is really *the* one?"

I shrugged.

"I'm not saying she isn't a great girl." She waved her hand. "This..."

"Kerrie," I said, raising my eyebrows.

"Fine, Kerrie," she continued. "I'm not saying Kerrie isn't a great person, but at your age, you have to keep your eyes and options open."

"I haven't really gone for the other options since we met."

"Like that matters. All men are like divining rods." She motioned to that bit of me beneath the tabletop. "That thing leads you all by the leash."

I conceded for the moment, recalling all the times before when I had tried to stay faithful because monogamy was "normal." But all of those other women were different, I told myself, despite the fact that I was well aware of my own reservations. I was being pulled between what I wanted and the person I had been, a person who took pride in how many notches he had in his belt.

It was about a week later when things between Kerrie and I fell apart. Well, a week until I sabotaged everything. Julian's and my mother's words ate at me, and I spent the week picking out her faults, like the scar on her knee from getting it scoped in college or the way one piece of her hair next to her ear couldn't be tamed with the rest. Things that had once been beautiful began to turn. Even her laugh started to get to me, and I felt suffocated. I wanted rid of her, and my betrayal was a foregone conclusion.

I went out with Julian, drinking through Saturday evening and into the wee hours of Sunday, having told Kerrie I needed a guys' night out. Despite that, I'd spent much of the night thinking of her. I threw back all the whiskey I could get my hands on, and it was getting late when I struck up a conversation with a woman a few years younger than Julian and me. She brushed against me in all the right ways, and I knew she wanted me. Julian grinned and gave his nod of approval when I left him at the bar with the same little blonde. I can't say I even remember her name. She wanted to get drinks back at my place, and I said yes, not thinking about anything but the moment. Maybe I wasn't thinking at all.

We had a few more beers in my living room before going into the bedroom, where, within a few seconds, we had shed our clothes as if they were an unnecessary skin, kissing and tangling with each other. But it wasn't happening. We groped and licked. I felt her growing wet, but I wasn't moving and wouldn't grow hard. Without even bothering to tug at it or let her try to work it herself, I simply apologized and blamed it on the whiskey, then we promptly fell asleep.

In the morning, when Kerrie stopped by to surprise me with the hangover cure, as she called it, of fresh bagels, lattés, and a back massage, she discovered us in bed. I leapt to my feet when I heard the bag of food crash against the wall, the scorching foam of the lattés coming across my face and body as the cups burst against the headboard. I cursed and hollered something, then realized what was happening only in time to hear the door slam shut behind her. By the time I could dress and get to the living room window, she was already in her car, speeding away. I turned around to see the spare key to my apartment on the coffee table next to the empty beer bottles from the night before.

She never forgave me, and I can't say I blame her. We talked about it on the telephone for the next few days, dragging things out as people tend to, but in the end, she admitted that she just couldn't get past it. I tried to say anything and everything I could to win her back the final time we spoke. But nothing worked. There wasn't a thing I could do. She really loved me, and I had hurt her as badly as any man can hurt a woman. I didn't deserve her and knew it, but in the end, I was overcome with helplessness and anger, so I yelled at her for crying, then slammed down the phone.

At the time, I chalked up losing her to one of those things men do, one of those mistakes we make when we're drunk. Maybe I had been afraid, letting what my mother and Julian had said get to me. Either way, she was gone, and I was alone again.

I wouldn't say that I miss her to this day, but she is still there, living in a photograph I have in a box of old things. In the picture, she's dipping her bare feet into the fountain across the street from Union Station. Her chestnut hair is coming across her face, carried on the wind, and she is smiling.

CHAPTER 20

NESTING

Julian finally went to Maria, the woman who had once been his occasional screw and, more recently, his stalker. She had hunted him down like a dog but had never managed to get her claws into him. That is until conscience intervened. Not his conscience, of course, but mine. I still have faith in the man, though, and like to think he would have gone to her and done the right thing even if I hadn't confronted him.

I don't find myself to be impossibly optimistic or blindly naïve when I admit that I see the potential for good in Julian. It's true that you could organize an entire hate group of women who don't have much faith in my friend, but he's capable of doing the right thing, of being genuine. After all, he went to Maria, turning up at her door on Wild Plum Avenue. He knew she had every right to slap him across the face, to call her Chicano cousins and brothers to come beat him within an inch of his life. But she didn't. Nor did she throw her arms around him when she opened the door, hugging him tightly because he had finally become the man and father who would help her raise this child. You know, the stuff of movies. No, instead she did the human thing, the natural thing.

When Maria answered the door, her arms fell to her side, and a steady stream of tears began to streak her face. She had been alone, desperate, and afraid. But Julian was there now, biting his lower lip as he stood awkwardly before her. The past eight months of aches and discomfort, coupled always with the insult of having to explain repeatedly why she was alone. Why there was no father by her side. All of that anger and fear and torment that had most certainly boiled up inside of her came pouring out with merely a glimpse at Julian's tender, sympathetic, and apologetic face. He knew he had wronged her and did everything to express how now, after all of this time, he was going to do the right thing.

"We're restarting things slowly," he explained to me when we got together only a few days after our argument at Café Napoli.

For many friendships, there might have been some blowback, a bit of repercussion, or even a period of silence. But Julian had called me the very next day to tell me he had an extra ticket for a midweek matinee baseball game. It was, I think, his way of apologizing.

"And yet she's already moved in?"

He turned to me with a look of depth and sincerity I hadn't before noticed in him, then said, "I'm only thinking of the baby."

A foul ball was popped up into our section of the stands, and we, along with a hundred other people, jumped up, nearly spilling our beers, in the hopes we might get our hands on it. The ball sailed over our heads. I turned to watch a father rise up above the reaching crowd a few rows behind us, balancing himself on a narrow plastic stadium seatback to snatch it from the air. He handed it to his son and was surrounded by applause.

"You're willing to marry this gal just for the baby?" I asked him as we settled back into our seats. "That's quite the one-eighty considering you ran from her for eight months."

"Don't say it like that," he said, putting his spin on the way things had happened in that beautiful way only Julian could. "And I'm not talking about marriage. I just don't want her to live in that shitty apartment all by herself. It isn't healthy. What if something happens?"

"That's a good point, I guess. So when you say you're taking it slow, does that mean you two haven't…?" I made a sophomoric gesture with my hands.

"Of course we have."

Though we were sitting elbow to elbow with other Cardinals fans that could all eavesdrop if they chose, we spoke candidly as if there weren't another soul around.

"Wow," I said. "That has to be something. She's huge. How do you go about getting around that?"

"Yeah, it isn't easy. I go at it from behind, which is the only way to really make it happen because it lets me enjoy it with my eyes open."

"You've been closing your eyes?"

"I have to," he said. "I can't keep it up if I'm staring at that big-ass belly and thinking about the baby I'm likely poking in the forehead."

I laughed. "Then why are you doing it in the first place?"

"Obviously she's crazy, Brett. Her hormones are all over the place. If I don't have sex with her, she starts going on and on about how she's ugly and fat and I could never love her."

"Christ."

"You have no idea," he went on. "Do you have any idea what nesting is?"

"I know what an empty nest is."

"Well, how do you think the nest gets filled in the first place? The bat-shit crazy mother bird buys thousands of dollars' worth of baby clothes and cleans the house over and over again. You know what I caught her doing the other day? Refolding all the baby clothes. She had pulled every last bib and onesie out of the drawers to reorganize and refold them. And when I asked her why she was panicking about how clean the house was, she snapped, yelling at me because the baby is coming and the house has to be spotless."

"It's not like the thing will even know the difference. You're not having company over for an elegant dinner. It's a fucking baby."

"I know! She's completely lost it."

"Do you think you will be able to handle all of this?" I asked, and regretted it. He had come so far, and I worried I was putting doubt in his mind.

He sighed and took another deep swig of beer. I signaled the vendor walking up the stairs for two more, and he obliged.

"To tell you the truth, Brett, I love that baby, and every day that passes, I love it more and more. I guess I've gotten used to the idea that I'm going to be a father. I mean, I'm still scared shitless. Literally. I haven't shit in three days. But when I look at her stomach, and I think about ball games and birthdays and teaching him to ride his bike, I almost break down crying because I'm so happy that I might burst."

"And Maria?"

"Bah! I can't fucking stand her," he said, then laughed. "With each passing day, I love my unborn son more and more, but I'm beginning to hate her. I have no idea what possessed me to take her out in the first place all those months ago."

A resounding crack echoed through the stadium as Albert Pujols's bat made contact with a hanging curve. The ball was sent arcing through the sky until it fell into the stands behind the bullpen. More than forty thousand people were on their feet, screaming and cheering as he rounded the bases. He clapped and whistled loudly as he pointed to the heavens to thank God for making him the greatest baseball player in the world.

Baseball is like church in that you jump to your feet in adoration and then fall back into your seats to let the magnanimity of greatness wash over you until that inspiration to arise stirs you once more. The only difference to me seems to be the absence of the kneeler, the scoreboard instead of the crucifix, and the stadium lights that have replaced the vigil candles.

"You said son?" I asked as we sat back down.

"We don't know for sure," he said. "She wants it to be a surprise. But I feel bad calling him or her an 'it' or a 'thing.' Just doesn't feel right."

I watched the ball, a blur of white, leave the pitcher's hand and streak away from the mound like lightning. Scott Rolen whipped the bat around, a lumberjack chopping down an oak, and hit nothing. From our seats, you could hear the clap of the ball striking the leather of the catcher's mitt as the crowd let out a groan of disappointment because the inning was over.

"Strangest thing," Julian said. "She's picked out everything for the nursery, down to the pictures of us in the mobile hanging above the crib. She has free rein over one of my credit cards and has spent God knows how much. But out of all her neuroses and illogical bullshit, there is one thing she truly doesn't seem to care about."

"What's that?"

"The baby."

"So you guys haven't picked out any names yet?" I could feel the afternoon drunkenness taking over and shuddered as a breeze cooled my cheeks.

"No," Julian said. "I've picked them out. She seems indifferent."

"And?"

"Well..." He licked his lips after a sip of beer. "I was thinking that, for a boy, I would like to name him after my father. And me, I guess. Since it's my given name, too."

"Baby Gabriel," I said, letting the name roll off my tongue and nodding in approval. "I like the sound of that. And what about for a girl?"

"For a girl"—he turned to me with that shit-eating grin of his—"I was thinking Brett might work."

"One of the greatest female literary characters of the past century," I reminded him.

I had always told him too much, opening up and putting myself out there the way women, not men, do. But there was always that occasional reward. Such close friendships might warrant complete honesty. He was my best friend after all, and, truth be told, I had been named after a woman, not a baseball icon. So on that sunny day, I was happy to hear he was considering honoring me and making me a part of his legacy. I had always been self-conscious about being named after a woman, but what did it matter, really? My name and the awkwardness that accompanies being named after someone of the opposite sex could live on in Julian's little girl. He had probably been chiding me on that day the Cardinals played the Pirates, but it didn't matter. It felt good to mean that much to him.

There was plenty of daylight left when the game ended. Once Julian and I left the stadium, we walked north on 7th, paying homage to the bronze figures of our heroes. I suppose that I was wobbling a bit, but it wasn't enough to slow me down, rather just the right amount to make me feel good.

Before the first pitch of every Cardinals game, the mob has purpose. A swarm of thousands walk shoulder to shoulder, tickets and baseball gloves in hand, filing through the turnstiles and hiking up the ramps to their respective sections. Red, gray, and white Cardinals-loving Americans, the greatest fans on Earth. When the game is over, though, it is a different scene altogether. After the ninth, everyone scatters. The gates of Busch Stadium leak like a sieve, bleeding fans out into the streets. Some go straight to their cars, those with children and happy homes to return to. The rest of us take no time getting to J. Buck's on Clark or trekking up north to Olive. If our boys have won, the throngs of fans spreading out in all directions from the stadium are filled with drunken chants. If we lost, the sounds are the same, though there is a guttural inflection, a bit of hatred and anger even. On that afternoon, slurs of victory, men and women randomly chanting "Cardinals!" and following it up with out-of-breath cheers and shouts, surrounded us. Julian and I were walking smack in the middle of countless people just like us, drunk and in love with a baseball team.

"I'm starving," I said as we crossed the street and continued north on 8th, daydreaming of a steak, medium-rare, and a vodka soda or perhaps a tall glass of red wine.

My favorite part of afternoon games was always how they ended just in time for happy hour or dinner. I wasn't following Julian as he took a left on Walnut, but I wasn't going anywhere on my own either. I didn't have any plans for us, just hopes for our customary dinner and more drinks. But instead, Julian took me by surprise by saying that he'd better be going home.

"I figured you'd want to drink some more," I protested. "Get dinner downtown or on the Landing, the way we always do."

"Not tonight," he said. We were outside the parking garage on the corner of 10th, and he actually paused to look at his watch. "I've got to get home. Maria will want something to eat. She has been craving tuna lately. I read the mercury levels are risky, and she's not supposed to have too much, but she won't listen. The house reeks of it."

I told him I understood, although I really didn't, and we embraced, giving each other that pat on the back that men do when they hug. Then he walked away, disappearing into the parking garage.

The baby was almost human-looking by now, growing inside Maria, surrounded by dim red light. I could picture little Brett or Gabriel in my mind's eye as I walked. In utero, a child looks like an alien for the most part, the Star Child from *2001: A Space Odyssey*. The baby would be with us soon. I knew it was to be a great thing, but I was in a sad place, torn up over the whole thing. I had wanted my friend to grow up. I had wanted us to be men. And now it was actually happening. Julian was doing it, first like nearly everything else, and I was left trying to catch up.

I considered a drink in this bar or that and desperately needed to piss, but I kept on walking, hoping to sober up enough to remember where I had parked. I laughed at myself. Nearly thirty years old and I was all alone, wandering the streets of a hometown I was too drunk to recognize, looking for my car until I remembered I had ridden the Metro.

As despondent as I was, I have to say that the decision I made in that drunken moment to pop in on my mother for a surprise dinner couldn't have been further from helpful. A rational, sober man would have known better.

I love my mother—after all, she is my mother—but she doesn't exactly exude sympathy and understanding. So it was strange that, as I left the Metro stop and found my car in the Central West End where I had left it, I should recall only the times she would reassure me and tell me everything was going to be all right even though it rarely ever was.

Once I reached Sutton Avenue, I parked on the street and walked up the sloping front yard, skipping the sidewalk altogether. The grass was neatly manicured, the lawn service I was paying to come out each week having cut it into little checkered rows just like the outfield at Busch. How I had hated mowing that damn lawn. It was only a small patch of green sod, but it signified the lost summers of my teenage years. My mother had wanted it cut, and, as she never tired of reminding me, a good son mows the lawn for his mother. She had cared so much about how it looked that she made me toil in that godforsaken turf for hours on end while my friends were doing whatever the hell they wanted.

Mother was sitting at the kitchen table, barricaded by books and papers, flipping through a novel. It was the same country-style kitchen table where, often in tears, I had learned to read at the age of six. Using her own harsh teaching method, she would grip the back of my neck and make me sound out every word, then recite their definitions.

"It is never enough to know a word," she would say. "You have to know how to use it too."

The linoleum floor of the kitchen, an off-white color with the forgiveness of vulcanized rubber, was the same as when I was a boy. The cabinets were white, the table wood, the curtains above the stainless steel sink nothing short of hideous. Nothing matched. Everything was scratched and beaten up over the years, but it still worked, so why replace it? I realized in that moment that my mother was the only thing in the room that had visibly changed. She had swollen and gotten old in the middle of it. I had grown too, of course. I wasn't the little boy I had been, watching her read her books at that table. The kitchen had remained the same while we both changed, two dandelions growing out of a crack in a rock. And there I was, suddenly struck with sobriety as I looked down at her, reading glasses balanced on the tip of her nose.

"Hello, Mommy!" I called, "mommy" being a cutesy thing I did from time to time.

"Brett." She stood up, smiling. "I didn't hear you come in." She held a lit cigarette in her hand outstretched far from my face, the smoke floating up from the tips of her fingers toward the recessed lighting on the ceiling, and wrapped me up in a hug with her right. She was smoking (again), a telltale sign that she didn't care much anymore. Why give a shit or make an effort if there isn't much worth making an effort for? She had nobody to impress.

"You look like shit, Ma," I said.

"I'm ready to go to bed." She was wearing a pair of flannel pajama pants and a Billiken's sweatshirt, likely old enough to be from my days at

SLU. It may have been summer outside, but she always kept the house as cold as a meat locker. She returned to her seat and said, "There's beer in the fridge. How was the game?"

"Great." I popped the top on a Bud Light and let the refrigerator door fall shut, the suction of the seal smacking as it closed. "We won."

"How's my second son?"

That was Julian. With the amount of time we spent together as boys, she had encouraged him to call her Mom, as his mother did for me. She had never been much of a fan—of Julian's, I mean—but she loved him anyway. It might seem strange for anyone to love someone like Julian. He has been and probably always will be a bit of an asshole. But he's our asshole.

"He's doing well." I sat across from her. She looked up at me. Her crow's feet creased away from her soft eyes toward her coarse, tangled hair. Maybe she really was ready for bed, lounging casually about the house, dressed for comfort. But her haggard look went beyond that. I had never seen her looking so old.

"And the baby?"

"Fine, fine," I went on. "You know, I never would have thought Julian could ever love anyone as much as he loves himself."

She asked me if I was hungry, and I told her I could eat.

"You know," she said as she banged around in the cabinets for a plate to microwave some leftovers, "I love that boy like he was my own, but sometimes he behaves like a real prick."

"We all do," I admitted.

The food in the microwave popped, cheese sizzling, sausage bursting.

"Ain't that the truth," she said.

The ding announced that it was time to eat, and she brought over my dinner, steaming. It was a dry mix of whipped potatoes and Polish sausage and a few slices of Cecil Whittaker's pizza, but I was too hungry to care. She had never been much of a cook, but she had always kept me fed.

The standards when I was growing up had primarily consisted of Shake 'n Bake or fish sticks served with macaroni and cheese. Everything is a rush when you're being raised by a single mother. I was always late for school, which meant she was late for work, and there was always something to be done that was more important than good cooking: laundry, lunches to pack, rooms to clean. Our house was consistently filled with projects left undone because there was never any time to complete anything. Just getting by took all of your time. Children are meant to be raised by partners, and my mother never had the luxury of support. Sure, my grandfather gave her a job and a bit of money, but beyond that and the brief stint with Gloria Brown, my mother and I were alone.

I ate and had another beer. She went on smoking, ashing her cigarettes into an old coffee mug. We talked about the game a bit more, glossing over Julian here and there, but never really giving it the attention I had intended. In time, I forgot about all of it and actually found myself enjoying the company of my mother, sitting at the kitchen table in our usual spots and laughing.

Within an hour, I had amassed a little aluminum castle of empty beer cans stacked like a wall that mirrored her bastion built of stacked papers and books. I moved from my usual spot at the table and sat next to her. The smoke wafted across my face on its way up toward the faded white ceiling. My mother noticed that it bothered me, so she stamped it out.

I leaned across the table, sifting through the old junk mail and bills. One of the stacks of books had some Henry James, a copy of *The Alchemist*, and some obscure tome by Melville, an author who had made it his life's work to examine the unbridled sardonic darkness of mankind versus a fable about the power of undying optimism. She was anything but predictable.

"Is this a romance novel?" I asked, holding up a hardback Danielle Steel novel.

"Yes." She snatched it from me. "I'm thinking of writing a paper discussing how the masses enjoy, actually enjoy, purchasing formulaic works that they have read over and over again."

"Bullshit," I said, calling her out.

The bit about the paper might have been true since she was always writing papers, literary academia having become her sick hobby. There are professors out there on tenure tracks, publish or perish situations, who would hang themselves if they found out a single mother in St. Louis had written papers for the hell of it and had gotten them published in journals across the country.

"So how are things at work?" She pushed the book aside and changed the subject.

"The usual," I said, continuing my rummaging. "I just effectively lied to millions of people, convincing them that fuel made from corn in Nebraska will save the world for their children."

"Good for you." She walked to the refrigerator again and got two beers this time, one for each of us.

At the bottom of one of her stacks, the one nearest the edge of the table, I found a few old photo albums. I sat back in my chair, crossing my legs, and I placed one on my lap and took a long drink as I flipped through the photographs.

"Is this me?" I asked, examining a photograph of an infant in the bathtub, naked as the day he was born, looking back over his shoulder and smiling up at the camera. My hair was a lighter shade of blond back then.

She leaned in and nodded. All the pictures were of me, baby me. My mother (and I assume the late, great Gloria Brown) had dressed me up in little suits, costuming me as a sailor even, my hair primped and styled. I'd never had a chance.

I closed the album and rose from my chair, taking my beer with me into the living room. The off-white carpet felt matted beneath my feet, and the chain on the lamp clinked as I pulled it, lighting the room with the muted yellow glow of an old bulb slow to warm up. I had spent so much time in that room, exploring every inch of that carpet, running my Matchbox cars and Micro Machines along the windowsills. My G.I. Joe's had base-jumped off the mantle, paratrooping into the Cobra Command center I had built at the base of the brick fireplace. The dull wood mantle was still covered with pictures in mismatched frames.

My mother had considered herself something of an amateur photographer when I was young, and the grainy Corwin family portraits were crowded to the back by her candid shots, in addition to all of my grade school class pictures. The one from third grade was the first to catch my eye. She had dressed me in a navy-blue suit and a paisley flower tie with matching pocket square. My hair was parted perfectly to the side. All the other boys and girls wore their regular uniforms, but I had to wear a suit and tie. I was like a doll for her sometimes, a thing she would dress up and groom however she liked. Second grade was next to fifth (chronology had never mattered much to my mother), and I wore a red bowtie and suspenders, a charming, albeit plastic, smile smeared across my face. She had blow-dried my hair that morning into a flowing coif. Think Zack Morris from Saved by the Bell.

As I walked down the line, studying each framed picture of myself, the repressed memories flooding back, I noticed a theme to everything my mother had chosen to display.

"Mom," I called out, finishing off the last of my beer. "What happened to all the pictures of me from high school and college?"

"They're around somewhere."

"Not that I can see," I said, walking back through the kitchen to the hall, where more pictures of her and me had been framed and hung on the walls. I wasn't over the age of twelve in anything.

"They have to be around here somewhere."

She was looking on her own now, leaning over a group of frames on a table in the entryway, a table I had knocked over a handful of times when I had come home drunk as a teenager. I had never before realized how many goddamned pictures that woman had framed all over the house. It was like a gallery filled with the worst art imaginable, an exhibition nobody had heard of or gone to.

"Mom, there is nothing here of me after the age of twelve. You know I was a teenager and became a man, right?"

"Yes, yes, of course," she said, laughing.

"You just don't like to be reminded of such things?" I met her at the kitchen table with two more beers.

"It's not that. To be honest, I guess I just like remembering you as you were." She pinched my cheeks, deliberately mocking the motif she was embodying. "My cute little angel."

"So I wasn't your cute little angel after the age of twelve?"

"You hit puberty." She said it so matter-of-factly.

"Huh." I had to keep on drinking. Her complexes and idiosyncrasies had lost most of their novelty for me, but she had still made an inquisitive, imaginative son out of all of that reading. "So you liked me better when I was a little boy?"

"Not better." She was smoking, and we had to talk through it. "I still love you, but I have a fondness for the way things were when you depended on me."

Coming from my mother, this bordered on sweet, so I let it all slide and appreciated her in that moment for who she was. We continued on for a bit longer at the kitchen table, building up our beer can forts. Then she said she was getting tired, which I took to mean she was feeling a bit drunk.

She had done her best to raise me right. That much was certain. It's true I had resented her the way children resent their parents. When the day came and I was given the chance, I would do it all differently. I had no idea how, but my children would love and appreciate me. She was a good parent, a good mother and father to me, but I vowed to do better if I ever had children of my own.

In the dim light of the hallway, she looked young again, and when she suggested I stay the night in my old room, a shrine that hadn't been altered since I had moved into Griesedieck Hall for college, she looked up at me so proudly that I knew that I loved her the way men love their mothers, and I told her so with a hug and a kiss on the cheek.

CHAPTER 21

THE ANGEL GABRIEL

One of the universally shared ironies in life is that not one soul can remember either of the two most important days of their life. Birth is a flash, a panicked, painful immersion of our undeveloped senses, while death is the climax when all those senses slip away from us, fading to black. The two most important moments, the entrance and the departure, are scarcely a blip, a footnote, while our first kiss or a last goodbye may remain with us for much of our lives. When it comes to our birth and death, it is other people, the people who share this minute existence in time and space with us, who are ultimately left behind with their cherished memories when we depart. And it is this fact, this indelible element of our humanity, which leads me to believe we may not be as selfish as we seem.

The day finally arrived for Julian's child to make their entrance into this world. Maria had come to full term, growing bigger than I ever imagined she was capable, though she still looked beautiful. But the glow was all on the surface, superficially coating a raging and unpredictable maelstrom of emotions and hormones. She was constantly hot and uncomfortable, and for the remaining month of her pregnancy, she had redirected her misery onto Julian, berating him endlessly even as he made his best efforts. Don't get me wrong. This was Julian, which called the quality of the effort into question, but the fact that he was making any effort at all was an admirable development for him. At least that's the way it looked from where I was sitting. And to me, it honestly didn't seem as if this was her way of punishing him for his disappearing act. Rather, it was simply her nature, a walking, talking live wire that would ignite if he had forgotten something she had asked for, looked at her as though she had lost her appeal, or so much as walked too heavily or pissed too loudly while she was trying to sleep.

Julian admitted to me that every day he was tempted to run again, to be rid of the whole mess. But thinking of the child, one all his own, would pull him back, providing the strength and will to stay. It was as if he had discovered a new sense of determination and resolve.

The thing about Julian is that, throughout his entire life, his success—with women, work, everything—had come naturally, effortlessly. When the going gets tough for people like that, they simply about-face and walk away. Even with a friendly competition between the two of us, anything from playing a bar game to making a pass at the same woman, whenever something would trouble him, he'd simply shrug his shoulders and claim he had never truly wanted it in the first place. If he didn't succeed from the start, he didn't want to play.

There was no walking away from this, however. Not for him. Not now. That feeling of love, true love for someone other than himself, had overwhelmed him. He was finally ready to create selfless memories, to form a space in this universe to be shared, to be cherished. He wanted to be loved despite his faults, to be respected because he had given life and was now a protector and provider. He wanted to be appreciated because, even though he was incredibly busy, he still took the time to play catch with his son in the backyard. He wanted to be remembered for all of these moments that were now possible. To put it simply, he wanted to be a good father.

People often need a second chance to do the right thing. The birth of Julian's child was like an absolution. He was given the opportunity to be a father, to move forward as if his absence for those initial seven months of the pregnancy didn't exist. Birth was a new beginning. It was time for Julian to begin looking to the future and making good on his mistakes. I'm of the opinion that righting your wrongs, correcting your own mistakes through your children, is in essence what parenting boils down to. Nobody gets it right the first time around, parents especially.

Julian got the opportunity for a second chance at being a good father. The pregnancy had been a mess for him, sure, and he had done all the wrong things. But at twenty-two minutes after three o'clock in the afternoon on Friday, September 12th, he was given another shot.

Maria's water had broken sometime before five o'clock in the morning, and she was still out cold when Julian awoke to a wet bed. He nudged her and then, as the gravity of the situation dawned on him, they both naturally panicked.

In the month that Julian and Maria had been living together in Frontenac, they had monitored Maria's every change closely. The baby felt lower in her pelvis, her heartburn and breathing improved, her discomfort and backaches increased, and she urinated constantly. The two had done plenty to prepare, attending a few Lamaze classes and the last of her prenatal visits. They had read *What to Expect When You're Expecting* and packed an overnight bag for the hospital filled with enough clothing and toiletries to last them a month. And yet, when the moment came, when they awoke to sheets soaked in amniotic fluid as the first of Maria's contractions kicked in, they remained anything but calm and rational.

Instead, frantic and hurried, they rushed about the house. Julian dressed in the dark and put on two different shoes. Maria scrambled to find her jacket and screamed at Julian for hanging it in the front closet. They remembered the bag they had packed for the hospital but forgot to change the bedsheets, leaving them to dry and crust. And then, as Julian backed out of the garage, he didn't give the door enough time to rise above the roof of the car. The screech of metal twisting and scraping filled the car, and Julian cursed but kept on reversing, determined to rush Maria to the hospital.

According to Julian, the light of day hadn't yet crested the Mississippi River, and as they sped through the empty early morning streets, an unseasonably cold autumn mist enveloped the city and gray light cut through the trees. The labor wouldn't begin for hours, possibly even an entire day, and yet he opened up his A8, roaring north on Ballas, rushing toward St. John's Mercy, where his child would be brought kicking and screaming into this world.

He had called and told me to meet him at the hospital, but by the time I had showered and made my way across town, Maria was already in labor and delivery. I met Julian in the waiting room, where he sat in an uncomfortable chair, unable to relax, his foot tapping on the shiny tile floor. It was seven o'clock in the morning.

Julian said my name as he rose from his chair to give me a hug. I patted him on the back, and we parted, smiles smeared across our faces. This was the moment, that meaningful instance shared by best friends, by brothers. There were no words necessary to tell him how proud I was of him, how happy I was for what was to come.

Directly across from us sat a broad-shouldered, weather-beaten Latino with full cheeks and a thick mustache, sitting upright in his chair, his paunch rounding out his T-shirt and lipping over the top of his belt. His thick fingers were wrapped over the tops of his knees. His eyes were dark, coal black even, and they were fixed on Julian.

"Oh," Julian said nervously. "Brett, this is Mr. Morales, Maria's father."

I rose from my chair and met him with my firmest handshake. His bear paw crushed my tiny fingers with its calloused, harsh grip. He smiled, his white teeth peeking out from behind the plump lips beneath his mustache.

Morales. I couldn't believe it. I had known her a year, and this was the first time I had gotten the last name. I sat turning the name over in my head again and again. Maria Morales. It had a befitting, lovely ring to it. I wondered if they would give the baby Julian's last name or hers. I couldn't very well ask Julian then, for in that moment, he was staring down at the floor, tapping his right foot, then his left. He wore a brown loafer on one and a black wingtip on the other.

He looked up. "Brett? Um, would you mind running over to my house to grab me some clothes? I'm a mess."

His hair was in disarray, and he wore a wrinkled, inside-out T-shirt and cuffed jeans.

"We have a bag of clothes for the baby and Maria," he went on, "but nothing for me to change into. I would go myself, but I want to be here if anything happens."

I nodded. "Of course I will."

As Julian reached into his pocket to give me his house keys, a midwife approached. She looked to be in her early forties and wore lilac-colored scrubs. Her shoes squeaked on the floor as she walked briskly through the waiting room toward Julian, who had already jumped to his feet. He stood with his arms folded, listening intently as she told him that Maria was six centimeters dilated with regular contractions, and it would likely be a few more hours before she progressed into full dilation and delivery.

That was when I noticed that there were even more of Maria's family members in attendance, all sitting on the other side of the waiting room. She had two dark-skinned brothers and two sisters there, all craning their necks and leaning over the backs of chairs to listen. The brothers were thin, one clean-shaven, the other sporting a mustache that matched his father's, while the sisters were plump, built like their father, visibly older than Maria, married, and probably with children of their own somewhere. The mother was missing, and I deduced that she was in the room with Maria, holding her daughter's hand and whispering encouragements into her ear.

I watched Julian as he leaned forward onto the balls of his feet, looking the midwife in the eye and nodding incessantly.

"Keys," I said to him when she had gone, my hand outstretched and waiting.

"Huh?" He turned to me, a look of distraction in his eyes. "Oh, no, don't worry about that. It's no big deal." He fell back into his chair and leaned back with a deep exhale.

"Are you sure? I really don't mind."

"Yeah," he said, putting his hand on my shoulder, and another, brighter, smile came across his face. "I'd rather have you here."

Quiet hours passed. Other women—imminent mothers—entered with their husbands and families to be wheeled off by nurses. Most husbands accompanied their wives, following closely behind the nurses pushing the wheelchairs, through the double doors to the back corridors where children were pushed into this world to take their first screaming breaths. I tried to picture what was happening back there, though my imagination could go no further than what I had seen on television sitcoms and that video they made us watch in biology class. My mind's eye was restricted by my inexperience, polluted with flowery pop culture and that one outdated documentary in high school that resulted in sophomoric groans and mock vomiting from the class.

Mrs. Reyes, Julian's mother, arrived at noon, looking a bit like Jackie O. Though her blue dress was somewhat dated, she wore it with grace and charm. Her auburn hair, marred only by a few gray streaks, was full and wrapped beneath her chin. This was an occasion, to be sure, and she had dressed for it. It had been nearly thirty years since she had brought her only son into this world, but it was obvious she knew there would be time, time to prepare for her first grandchild to make his or her grand entrance.

She took Julian in her arms and fought back the happiest of tears. They exchanged some close words, sharing and acknowledging this special moment in time as Julian and I had done. I hugged her as well and then returned to my seat to watch her meet, one handshake at a time, the Morales family. This was a big day for everyone present, and these two families were coming together, expanding whether we liked it or not.

My mother followed some twenty minutes later, arriving with a little less grace and asking first for directions to the restroom. Returning with wet hands, she expressed congratulations to both Mrs. Reyes and Julian with her trademark hugs that lasted too long, then took the seat next to me and reached over the armrest to take my hands in hers before digging through her oversized purse for a book of crossword puzzles.

The excitement faded as we leaned into the unknown number of hours that still had to pass. The waiting room was typical: a fish tank, flowered chairs with uncomfortable wooden armrests, soothing eggshell-blue walls, old magazines, and a flat-screen television mounted high above our chairs. I had nothing to read, so I took in the room, every detail, every person who came or went. Eventually, I had to join in with Mr. Morales and the rest of Maria's family, the lot of us staring up, hypnotized by daytime television.

The Morales sisters were enamored by the soap operas, changing seats to place themselves directly in front of the television, while the patriarch lost interest quickly and fell asleep in his chair, the fold of his thick neck rounding out beneath his chin. I found myself increasingly impressed by his mustache, a wide and dense push broom. The brothers—Maria's tall younger brothers who, if I had to guess, were scarcely twenty—had an air of mischief to them, looking boyishly as they wandered in and out of the waiting room. It seemed they were exploring the hospital, laughing and enjoying their wait. In all, the family seemed disinterested, though that should be expected. For Julian and me and our mothers, this child was our first addition, but for the Morales family, it was just another niece or nephew, another grandchild to continue the expansion of their already large family.

I rather respected Maria's family, appreciating them for the way they interacted with each other. They looked and acted like a real family, touching shoulders and sharing this time together. Occasionally, they spoke Spanish to one another or as a collective group, laughing at some private little quip or speaking in a low, serious tone. Instead of finding it rude, I felt their closeness was endearing. I doubted they were having private or scheming talks but rather that they were expressing themselves the way they had as children, as a family. In that moment, as I sat face-to-face with this tightly knit and complete family, I considered what family actually meant.

I looked at my mother, reading glasses on the tip of her nose, her eyes working the crossword puzzles, indifferent to the world around her. Julian's mother was seated on the far side of her. She hadn't bothered to set down her purse. It was still on her lap, her hands folded over the top of it, and she remained composed and proper next to her son, who sat fidgeting. It looked as though he were still a child, waiting for the pediatrician to call him back. So much time had passed since Julian was a boy, a child, and though they had come so far, it was touching to sit there and observe how little had really changed.

Hours ticked by before a nurse appeared donning a bright and cheery disposition despite the long hours on her feet. We often forget that, for those like her, this child wasn't life-affirming or a catalyst for change or growth in any way. No, this baby, like all the other children she brought into this world, was merely the order of the day, another in a long line.

"Congratulations," she said to Julian. "You're the father of a baby boy."

Julian brought his palms together and closed his eyes. I had never seen him pray before. The waiting room had slowly filled with other families, and everyone began their congratulations. Julian turned and again wrapped his mother in his arms. The Morales boys cheered, and the sisters joined and then looked as if they might cry out of happiness as their father hugged them and rubbed their backs with his massive, calloused hands.

Then, after a moment, the Morales family crossed the waiting room and each sister embraced Julian's mother and then Julian in turn. One by one, the boys shook Julian's hand. Finally, it was the patriarch's turn. I watched as the stern father approached Julian's outstretched hand only to pat it aside and instead wrap his massive arms around this young man, enfolding him tightly and lifting him off the ground as all was forgiven.

"Mother and son are both doing fine," the nurse announced when quiet reigned again. "I'll take you back if you're ready to meet him."

Julian followed the nurse down the hall, passing an exhausted-looking Mrs. Morales on their way. She smiled at him and touched his shoulder but seemed to do so with far less familial enthusiasm than the others. Rejoining her husband and adult children in the waiting room, Mrs. Morales settled into a chair and sat quietly. The rest of us followed suit, and for the first time I started to get frustrated with how anticlimactic this all was starting to feel.

I must have nodded off at this point and am not sure how much time passed. Julian had returned and stood before us, poised and ready to make an announcement.

"His name is Gabriel," Julian said, taking his mother in his arms and dancing with her for a moment. "Gabriel Reyes—after me and my father and my father's father."

"Well," his mother said, "let's go meet my grandbaby already."

"You'll have to wait your turn," Julian said. "Let's go back there now, but I haven't even gotten to hold him yet."

"What?" I asked. "The wait must be killing you."

"It is," he said, "But the moment I got back there with the nurse, some gal from the hospital forced her way in and made sure we got our paperwork done. She was eager to get to the weekend and we were the last one on her list."

Julian led his mother by the arm down the hall and the rest of us followed, a strange menagerie of two overgrown boys and their mothers being trailed by a large Latino family. Arriving at the room, Julian turned to us and measured the crowd following him.

"I have no idea what the rules are at this point, but I doubt we can all fit in there," he said. "Squeeze in as many as you can, I guess."

Entering the room, Julian approached Maria and the child sleeping on her chest as she rested on the inclined hospital bed. Wrapped in blue swaddle blankets, baby Gabriel was smaller than I had expected, a petite little bundle in a stocking cap. Julian encouraged Maria to turn him around, to show him to everyone.

"The nurse said he has a full head of hair already," Julian said. "I have to see it."

Maria tried to stop him, but Julian pulled off the stocking cap to reveal a tuft of blond, curly hair that matched the fair skin. The child, as if on cue, opened his bright blue eyes to welcome us.

"He seems a bit light, doesn't he?" My mother, with that characteristic inability to shield honesty, spoke first from the doorway.

She was right. The child was blond, blue-eyed, and Caucasian in a way that defied both Reyes and Morales. They were both dark, hair bordering on black, eyes the saturated color of good earth. He should have been brown, beautifully dark as they were.

Within moments, a gulf expanded between our odd little family and the Morales clan. The sisters and brothers turned away with their mother and father and began to hurl little bits of Spanish at one another.

Julian backed away from Maria and the child, confused, open-mouthed. He turned to me, examining my fair hair and light eyes.

"Don't look at me," I said honestly as I self-consciously touched at my sand-colored hair. "I never touched her."

And with that, things truly began to fall apart. Something was so obviously wrong, so evidently out of place.

"It isn't his," one of the sisters broke her vow of Spanish.

Julian turned from the child and Maria to me, his eyes watering with a hate and sadness I could almost touch. He started toward the door and we parted for him. I was frozen momentarily, shocked in place by what I had seen. Looking over my shoulder, I watched Maria return the stocking to the child's head as she bit at her lip and self-consciously looked from her mother to her father.

I followed after Julian, weaving through the Morales family and then darting down the hall. He heard my approach and spun toward me, ferocity mixed with pain lining his face.

"I told you I wanted to wait!" he screamed, and shoved me backward with a strength I didn't know he had. It was the only place all that anger, all that embarrassment and hurt, could go.

As he stormed off, I wanted desperately to call after Julian. To tell him how sorry I was. To tell him that things would be all right. But I was on the floor, and I could only lie there and watch as he marched away in the mismatched shoes he had not cared to change because the birth of his son was more important.

I remember now that the hallway had grown silent save for the sound of Mrs. Reyes' inconsolable sobbing. My mother had taken her in her arms and turned to me.

"Her lack of character," she said, looking at me as she held onto the shaking shoulders of Julian's mother. "Never forget it."

CHAPTER 22

ANOTHER FATHERLESS SON

What were the chances, the odds, of that boy coming out fair and with blue eyes? Maria was dark, to be sure, with her year-round tan and thick, near-black curls, while Julian had a Spanish father. I don't remember much about Gregor Mendel and those little boxes from grade school science class, but I figured that if the child were Julian's, the newborn should have emerged with even the slightest hints of that Hispanic American beauty that both Julian and Maria embodied. But it was those strong recessive genes, the ones that belonged to his true father, that had overtaken the boy in utero, developing him into an angel that had none of Julian, nor of the namesake printed on his birth certificate, inside of him.

Without those recessive genes, little Gabriel might have had a chance at a normal enough life—a life with a father. If he had looked even remotely like Julian, the assumption might have remained. Julian and Maria would have been miserable together for as long as they could stand it, then the child would have been shared between them, given the opportunity of both a father and a mother. Instead, Julian and everyone else jumped to that all-too-obvious conclusion—a conclusion that, in fact, turned out to be true—and when he stormed out of the hospital, the Morales family was left to care for their daughter and new addition.

What followed was, admittedly, quite childish. Maria and Julian began bickering and arguing over the telephone. At first, Julian called her incessantly, screaming at her for being a whore, claiming dishonestly that he had been faithful to her and that she had tricked him. Yelling back in turn, Maria expressed all the things she couldn't while they had been living together, often mocking his masculinity, which I know ate him from the inside out.

The real father was exposed to Julian during one of these screaming matches. He was a man named Dylan, a construction worker from Virginia who had lived in Maria's building. Dylan had left for home some months before little Gabriel's entrance, a departure that occurred all too closely to Maria's own realization that she was pregnant. It would seem she had hedged her bets.

As for her and Julian, he had money, she was desperate, and let's face facts: a Catholic girl with a family like that had few options. Once he returned to her, she must have felt more secure because he wasn't half the country away. And though he could never truly love Maria, a fact I believe she knew, at least he was willing to tolerate her for the sake of the child.

Unbeknownst to any of us, the events following Gabriel's birth proved that Maria felt the same disdain for Julian and was enduring his selfishness and chauvinism for the sake of her unborn child. Once the bottom had fallen out and it was obvious that Julian wasn't the boy's father, she was through with him. She wanted the boy's biological father, his real father. Why put up with Julian if she didn't have to?

Weeks went by. The baby was growing, centimeter by centimeter. He may have already lifted his head or watched objects for short periods. Julian, however, was witness, father, to none of this. And yet, in spite of the child not being his and the insults from Maria continuing to pile up, he still tried to break through, deciding that he could bear loving a child who wasn't biologically his. He wanted to be a part of that boy's life, and once Maria realized this, she knew she wielded power over Julian. It was her time for retribution, and so she tortured him, teased him with the potential for reconciliation between insults and arguments. But he remained steadfast, resolute, the love for the boy providing him with the strength he needed to carry the weight of Maria's abuses. This was, of course, a fleeting strength, one that eroded over time and eventually collapsed with a simple, quiet revelation.

During a lull, a quiet moment when it seemed they had nearly reconciled, Maria struck the final blow by admitting to Julian that, though she had begun the process of wiping his name from the birth certificate and changing the child's last name to Morales, she had decided to keep Gabriel as the first name. It's possible she may have expected this to appease Julian, or, and I find this more likely, maybe she knew it would be the ultimate insult, the one to push him from her life entirely. Whatever the motivation, he flew into a rage, the screaming and cursing beginning anew until she simply hung up.

And then there was silence. Julian continued to call, day in and out, chasing Maria as she had chased him, begging her to share the boy with him. He left voicemails until the mailbox was full and kept calling until the phone number was disconnected altogether. Following that, he tried to get through to her family, but they ignored him too. On the few occasions when his calls were met by the heavy accent of Maria's mother or sisters, he was promptly disconnected the moment he spoke. Mr. Morales, the one with whom Julian seemed to bond that day at the hospital, never picked up the receiver.

As for our relationship, Julian forgave me quickly for overstepping my bounds. After all, he needed me now more than ever. Save for his mother, he had no one else. And I remained in his corner, so to speak, consoling him as he made these incessant phone calls in a desperate attempt to be part of the boy's life. I had wanted to tell him he was going about it all wrong, that calling Maria names and stalking her family was getting him nowhere, but I had screwed things up enough already.

It was when Maria filed for a restraining order against Julian that things really became interesting.

Out of frustration, Julian sought legal recourse. What he found was a woman, an attorney named Gertrude Articola who specialized in family law for a giant litigating empire headquartered downtown. We chose her from the list of experts in family law for two reasons: first, she was expensive and, therefore, had to be good, and second, she was a woman, and we figured having a woman on our side might garner some much-needed sympathy.

"I see," she said when he announced that he wanted to obtain custody of his son. "How old is the child?"

"Only a month," Julian answered.

"And how long have you two been together?" she went on, glancing at me.

"No, no, you don't understand," Julian protested. "He's just my friend."

That didn't sound much better. She raised her eyebrows.

"I mean, we aren't together. Brett came along for moral support."

"Very well, Mr. Reyes," she said briskly. "What I need to know straightaway are the particulars."

There was something about the way she sat at that desk then, her arms wrapped in a cardigan and folded in front of her, that reminded me of being scolded by one of the nuns, those androgynous women who could cast a stare stern enough to keep your entire body clenched in your chair. I knew we had done nothing wrong. We were there for the right reasons. Julian wanted to do the right thing, but this woman was cold and calculating, an attorney.

I tried to settle in, but it felt like my suit—we both wore suits to that late Wednesday afternoon meeting—was bunching and sticking in all the wrong places. The club chair, one of a pair that faced Ms. Articola's desk, had looked comfortable, the tawny leather inviting, but the springs prodded me here and there. We were looking out over downtown from nearly twenty stories above St. Louis—up in the stratosphere, sealed inside a climate-controlled fortress, and we had to sit on something no more comfortable than the sidewalk.

"Well, my first advice in these situations is always to keep your relationship with the mother intact," she told Julian.

"Regrettably, it's too late for that." Julian had crossed his legs, his hands in his lap, and I realized that he was slipping into his role, confiding in his attorney, bearing his soul, and yet keeping a cool, reserved demeanor about him. If he hadn't kept himself in check, the entire thing might have become a game: the courtroom, the jury of his peers, the attention, him leaning in to whisper something to his attorney. Or perhaps I had seen too many movies.

"Understood." She wasn't annoyed yet, but I sensed she was getting there.

"Biologically, you see," Julian started in, and Ms. Articola picked her head up from where she had been jotting notes, "the child isn't mine. He's someone else's. But when Maria told me she was pregnant, I had to come to grips with fatherhood. It took me a long time, and it was difficult. But in the end, I decided to be a father."

"I see," she said. "Then you and the mother were sexually intimate during the possible time of conception?"

"That's correct."

"Is there a blood test, one that has been weighed in accordance with the evidence of the statistical probability that you are the father?"

"No blood test was done," he said. "But you see, we didn't need it. All the while that Maria—that's the mother's name, Maria Morales—well, the entire time she was pregnant, it was assumed I was the father. She swore she'd been faithful to me, and she even got offended when I brought up the possibility. But when he was born, he didn't look like either of us."

"Infants often don't resemble their parents —"

"But we are both Hispanic from long lines of dark-skinned, dark-haired, dark-eyed people," Julian protested. "And he is blond and blue-eyed, fair-skinned too. It just didn't add up. Everybody there could tell he wasn't mine. I had already signed the birth certificate, already done the paperwork, before I had even had a chance to see him. I wasn't in the room when he was born. It very well may be that some children don't look much like their parents at birth, but this was not one of those instances. Since then, she has admitted she fucked around, told me who the real father is, and told me that I won't ever be part of Gabriel's life."

"The infant's name is Gabriel?"

"Yes." The name had brought Julian to the verge of tears. "We named him after my father. And me. Gabriel is my first name, too."

"I understand how difficult that must be, Mr. Reyes." Her tone was bereft of that icy numbness of before. It seemed his genuine nature had been able to soften her, to make her care.

"So —" he cleared his throat, cutting through that sliver of emotion he had let slip out "— what are my options?"

"Well, there are many different avenues we could take." She set her pen down. "This kind of thing isn't unprecedented. There was a case in the fifties, Fiege v. Boehm, in which a woman, Boehm, became pregnant and believed in good faith that Fiege was the father. Fiege agreed to financially support the child and to incur the birth expenses, covering these costs until a blood test revealed that he was not the father. Boehm, the plaintiff, sued and won because, as it turned out, it was immaterial whether the defendant was the father or not. He had agreed to pay based on Boehm's claim, which was made in good faith, that he was the father. Now, that pertains to our case because if we can prove that you were deliberately duped into believing you were the father, then you would be entitled to monetary compensation."

"But that's the thing," he said earnestly. "I don't care about the money."

"I thought you might not," she replied, breathing in deeply. "Which father's name is on the birth certificate?"

"Mine," he said.

"Then you were presumed to be the father," she said, seeming to have solved it just like that. "In this state, which is not unlike most, the court seeks to establish a family of two parents, a father and a mother. You, Mr. Reyes, certainly have a claim as the father since, in good faith, you acknowledged your paternity of the child and were named the child's father on the birth certificate."

"How do we proceed?" Julian smiled that wide Julian smile. For a moment, he had won; he had gotten the upper hand on Maria and was going to have exactly what he wanted, as always.

"This is where things tend to get a bit more complicated, Mr. Reyes. I understand your love for this child. I get a lot of parents in here, but I can see you are genuinely interested in what is best for him."

"I don't quite follow you."

"The issue isn't whether or not you have a claim to the child but rather how we should proceed with your claim." She said this with the air of someone about to give bad news. "You have no ties to this woman," she went on, "and in order to be a part of this child's life, you will have to support both the child and, from the sound of it, the mother, financially. But that is beside the point because even if you win shared custody, you have to be willing, after all the money you will spend fighting this woman, to be the second of two fathers. His biological father has a claim to him as well."

"And if he doesn't lay claim to him? What if he grows up without a dad at all?"

"That is something to consider as well," she admitted. "Though what it comes down to is the best interest of the child. Is it best for a child to have two different fathers and a mother? Is it best for a child to have a father figure who is forced to explain to him, at any given age, what their actual relationship amounts to?"

"But I love him," Julian fired back.

"I understand that. I truly do. But before we proceed, I have to know whether or not you honestly believe that the best interest of this child is to grow up shared between two different fathers, one of which, at the very least, has a relationship with the mother that is adversarial at best."

Julian wrung his hands together and looked down at his feet. I could almost sense a piece of him dying in that very moment.

`"Parenthood is about sacrifice, Mr. Reyes," she said, clearly determined to drive the point home. "And if you truly love this boy, then you have to consider what is best for him."

We walked out of the law office tower onto Olive, the clear late afternoon sun making shadow puppets of the skyline. The two of us turned east, buttoning our suit jackets to fight the autumn air. Neither of us spoke as we walked down the sidewalk with our hands deep in our pockets.

At the corner of 7th, we stopped at a liquor store. I bought us a six-pack of Budweiser and a bottle of cheap whiskey. It felt like an afternoon for cheap whiskey. We walked with it, wrapped loosely in a paper bag, turning south without a destination in mind or a care. I took a long, hard drink. My mouth filled with heat, and I choked down a campfire that flowed into my chest and warmed my stomach before sending a slight shiver through my arms and legs.

By the time we made it to Kiener Plaza, the two of us had passed the bottle back and forth a number of times. I wanted to stop but didn't say anything to Julian, whose eyes were focused ahead of him. The pedestrian mall stretched east, a long rectangular park the width of a city block consisting of pink brick walkways interspersed with manicured lawns and trees bearing russet leaves. At the center of the pergola was an oval pool, an empty fountain where, before the waters had been turned off for the season, a blue manmade river had flowed down steps and over rocks and then stilled at the bottom, where children would toss in their coins to make wishes. In the distance was the emerald dome of the Old Courthouse, Romanesque with brilliant white columns and a high American flag poking off the top of it. Framing it all stood the Gateway Arch, a dull silver in the fading light.

The plaza was empty that Monday afternoon, nearly desolate, and the dead, crackling stray leaves jumped and tumbled on the swirling winds as they snaked their way through downtown St. Louis. If the Cardinals had won anything meaningful, this is where the celebration would have been. All throughout the playoffs, there would have been rallies, and the fountains would all have been dyed red. This is where the World Series parade would have begun and ended. People would have flowed together in a beautiful mass of cheering and exaltations. But the Cardinals hadn't been good enough to even make the postseason. There was no ticker tape, no confetti, no celebratory dogpile on the cover of the Post-Dispatch. It was the beginning of October, and the season was over for us. At least in baseball, there's always next year.

We crossed Market Street. The flowery annuals of the median were turning, the decorative grasses browning. City landscapers would remove the dead flowers soon, then till and plant them anew in the spring. Mike Shannon's steakhouse was on our left. The stadium was ahead, the red brick rising up to ornate painted ironwork meant to resemble the Eads Bridge. It was beautiful, a marvel. We continued on silently toward it, drawn by it.

A vast empty gravel lot lay before us, the site of old Busch Stadium, now a flattened dust lot of uneven rock, guarded by thin chain-link fencing. I had seen my first baseball game there. It may have been an old and unsightly venue, but I loved it, off-white arches and all. I, along with the rest of St. Louis, had watched them tear it down, slamming into it with a wrecking ball rather than imploding it because they feared damaging the Metro. They had taken it down piece by piece and left fans with nothing but memories.

It seemed a pity that, after some years, the lot remained empty. Maybe Lally and Sons would buy the land and rebuild. Stadium living for the young and chic. They could fashion an entire area, a lifestyle, centered around the stadium. Bars and restaurants. City blocks that stirred all hours of the night, the streets filling and mobbing whenever we won. A place of celebration. Though, if I'm being perfectly honest, Julian and I are probably too far on in years to continue with that sort of lifestyle.

At the stadium entrance, we stopped. Julian leaned against the bulky pedestal of Lou Brock's statue. Putting his back against the black granite, he slid down, slumping onto the concrete beneath the towering stadium. I popped a can of beer and handed it to him. It was the only consolation I knew how to offer, and as we drank in silence, I wondered if it would always be like this, just the two of us for the rest of our lives, us and the statues of better men.

I watched as Julian reached into the breast pocket of his suit and fumbled with something out of sight. He made as if he were going to pull it out but instead hesitated, looked up at me for a moment, then dropped his hand. I turned away and tipped back my beer, giving him the privacy of silence. When I looked back to him, his beer was to his side and he sat staring at a small object in his fingers.

"You know, I've never told you," Julian started, "but I carry this for luck sometimes."

As I focused on the oblong piece of aged metal between his fingers, he flipped it gracefully into the air with his right hand and caught it with his left. I realized in that moment that it was the slug from World War II, the bullet Great Uncle Jack had given to Julian when he had drunkenly mistaken him for one of his own grandchildren. Julian began to turn it over and over and over again in his fingertips.

"I wanted to give it to my son one day," he went on, shaking away the timbre of emotion in his voice. "To make it a sort of family heirloom."

I told him I understood.

"It's stupid, I know. I mean, he wasn't even my grandfather. But he was a hero, you know? A great man," Julian paused. "At least that's what everybody always said."

We sat there in silence for what felt like hours, passing the whiskey back and forth a few more times. Then, I watched as he put the family relic back into his breast pocket.

"Julian," I said, "I know you don't hold much stock in these sorts of things, but a German poet named Schiller once wrote that 'It is not flesh and blood but the heart which makes us fathers and sons.'"

He looked up at me and simply nodded, admitting to me that he liked the sound of that.

"Do you think I would have been a good father?" he finally and inevitably asked.

"Honestly?" I said. "No, I don't."

He laughed and called me an asshole.

"The decision you made today leads me to believe you already are a good father, Julian." I touched his shoulder with one hand and tilted the bottle of whiskey back to take another drink.

"Thanks." He smiled up at me, but it was forced, hollow even, and fleeting. It was as if he would only allow himself the briefest of reprieves before focusing once again on his loss, on the moments he would never spend with his son.

Julian had tried to do the right thing—or at least what he thought was the right thing—for once. He had tried to make up for a lifetime of lost experiences by being a father, by loving Gabriel. Sometimes the right thing isn't all that obvious, though. Julian instead chose to sacrifice his own happiness with the hope that this boy would have a chance at something like a normal life.

And in that moment, as we sat in the shadow of Busch Stadium, drinking solemnly, I tried to believe in the possibility of such things. I tried, delving into the depths of my soul, to believe that Maria would be a good mother and the boy's father would move back to St. Louis for him and be all the things Julian and I had never experienced. But as I tried to manifest even a glimmer of optimism, I realized that I didn't have any remaining in there. It had all been swallowed up or thrown away.

Then, involuntarily, I pictured the boy. He's seven and standing in the middle of an empty baseball diamond, the one between Zephyr and Lyndover where Julian and I first became friends. The boy has a glove on one hand and is holding a baseball in the other. He's looking down at his feet, shuffling them on the grass. The stands are empty, the field desolate. There's nobody to catch the ball, nobody to throw it back. No, the boy is utterly alone, and it's clear he's been left that way, abandoned out there to grow up as confused as the rest of us.

*9 7 8 1 6 4 5 3 8 6 1 1 7 *